FOTOART

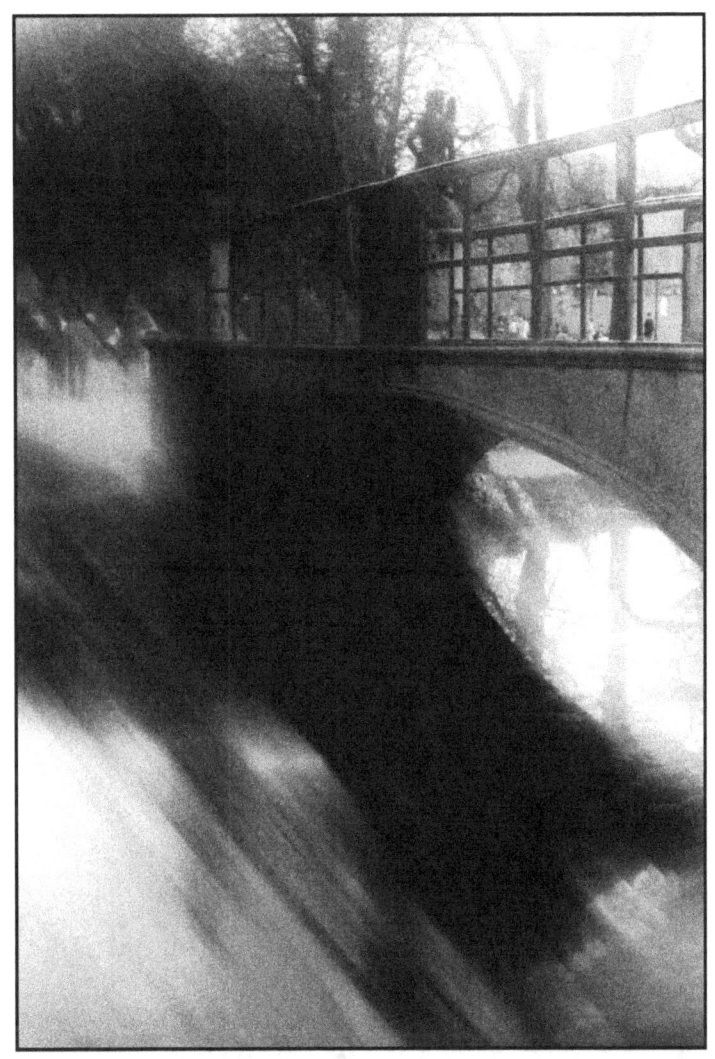

DOMENICO MURATORE

FOTOART

© - 2020 - All rights reserved
ISBN: 9798673345542
All images are the exclusive property of the author.
The images are produced from negative film frames

FOTOART

**To my children Massimo and Mattia
and my granddaughters Maya and Matilda**

FOTOART

*

Thanks

I thank my wife Irma who, with her patience, has allowed me to devote myself to my favorite hobby. Thank you for the love with which you have helped in my cultural wandering, giving me strength in moments of distrust, in showing me the way forward.

FOTOART

CONTENTS

	Acknowledgments	3
1	I remember…	7
2	My Milan	9
3	Rural civilization of Southern Italy	33
4	Symbolic photo	57
5	The extraordinary nature of simple things	71
6	Various photos	95
7	Author information	109

FOTOART

1 I REMEMBER...

Back in 1960, when I lived in Calabria, my parents gave me a Ferrania. It was a black plastic camera with a fixed lens. It allowed you to take photos with flash. This was its main feature. I remember that it was equipped with an openable silver umbrella in which you needed to insert special light bulbs to produce the flash. The hardest thing, then, was finding these light bulbs. My search extended to Cosenza. I found them in a small shop in the suburbs. How happy I was when I had them in my hands! I would have that camera at my complete disposal. I began taking photos: people, places, objects. I discovered a close and very different world. A world that, although familiar, was unknown to me. That tool made me embark on the path of an unusual creative art, based on seeing, perceiving subtle vibrations, discovering, sealing in time the pain and joy hidden in the folds of wrinkles, the smile of children happy with very little and the calm majesty of old age. School and the commitment that the teachers demanded allowed me to occasionally dedicate myself to my passion but... at the end of the school year, every moment was dedicated to my quest. I learned to develop negatives and positives in a photo lab. The only one in town. The owner, a shy man of few words taught me how to do it, with strange powders and strange mixtures, developers and fixing. It was a great wonder to learn that a precise variation in temperature would give my images the picturesque imprint.

I experimented, we experimented and... when he understood my fervent passion, he wanted to accompany me on my photographic excursions to shoot the beauty of useless things, the simplicity of a rural life, today gone.

One day he told me, "I'll show you photos I've never shown anyone." He opened an enormous cardboard box and out came photos of unprecedented beauty. I was amazed. The shades of grey, the perfect synchrony of the black and the white, the artfully managed graininess, the themes: tuna fishing, popular festivals, faces, made those images unique.

I realised that he was a true artist.

"You see," he told me, "If I was born in another place I would have had a future, but here I can't do anything but rejoice in what I have produced. Besides, nobody understands photography in this town. In order to live I have to things I don't like: photos of weddings, baptisms, birthdays. You want to compare the expressive face of this old woman with this wedding photo?" As he spoke, he pointed to a faded photo unsecurely stuck on a wall worn out by time.

"Why not do an exhibition?"

"Who would understand it!" he answered.

Maybe he was right! Sometimes, when I go back in time with my mind, I see that strange character who taught me the secrets of this art and I regret… not asking for a photo of him.

I think that if he had lived until now, with the marvellous tool that is the internet, he would have been able to share his secret and delicate aestheticism with us all.

After university, I chose to live in the city of Milan. Stunning city! I changed many cameras, took two enlargers, passed onto colour photos, I experienced pictorialism, but the memory of my first camera and my first teacher, the memory of my places, past worn out faces, and the creative moments I lived accompany me like a photo accompanies the moment it holds.

2 MY MILAN

What is more beautiful than feeling alive in a place where life flows at a hectic pace, where time seems to pass quickly and everything has to be done according to rules based on efficiency and dynamism?

Milan! Living in this city is living life. Modernity, the participatory attention towards beauty, cultural initiatives, the idea of the other and… a lot of discretion in a sea of traffic now orderly and unrestrained.

Milan! City of art in which you breathe the greatness of the past, in which the modern, made of taste and fashion, seems to be stuck like a label that is determined and defined even in the fluctuating tide of people who come and go, who run and stop, who watch and talk.

A wonderful, enchanted city, full of tremors, separated from conventional limits in which the free flow of existence is made for spirits who are inclined to receive the taste of life.

The freedom that is breathed in it is determined by incessant moments of attachment to the earth full of anxieties, tensions and sweet confusion but, also by the usual white of its sky and sometimes by its full blue, fantastic, clear and intense.

Those who live it, smell it, love it, respect it like you love and respect your own wife or the dearest thing to you.

The intense years of work, art and culture, lived fully in incessant rhythms of love, led me to find past momentsin my memory and to feel it inwardly, unique, beautiful and great.

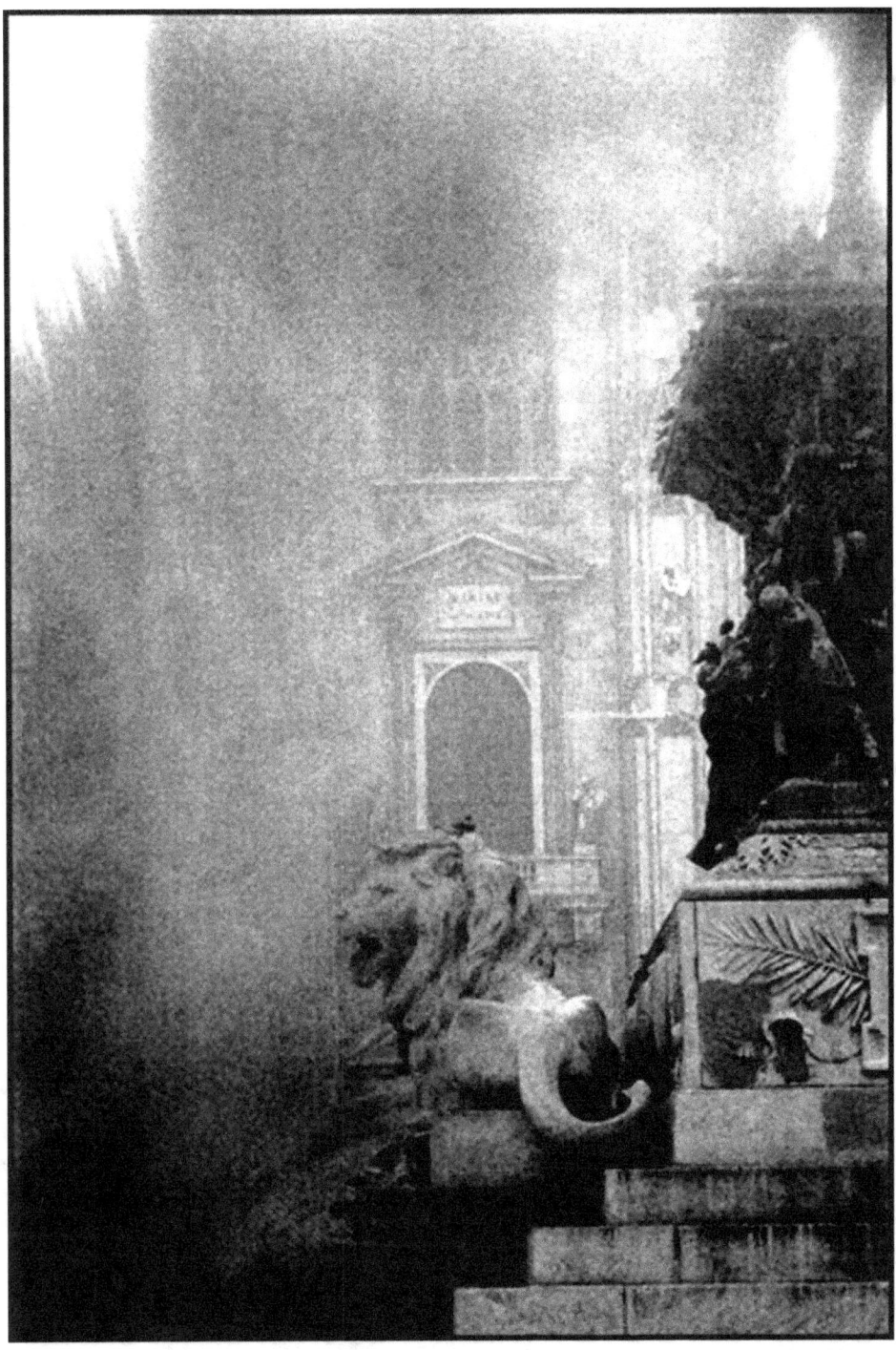

1982- Milan – Piazza Duomo – Olympus OM2 – Ilford HP5 – Devel. Kodak D76

FOTOART

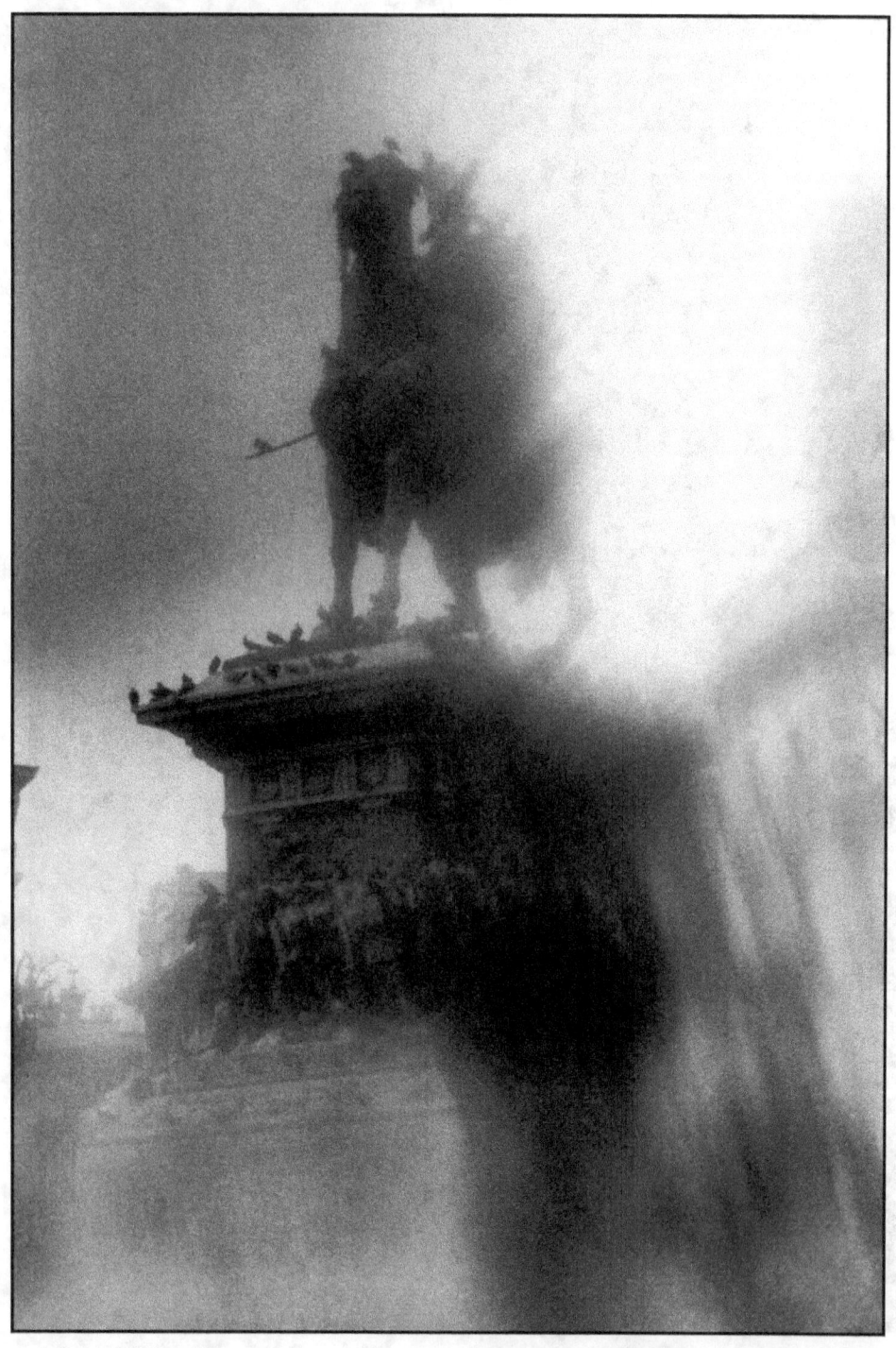

1982- Milan – Piazza Duomo – Olympus OM2 – Ilford HP5 – Devel. Kodak D76

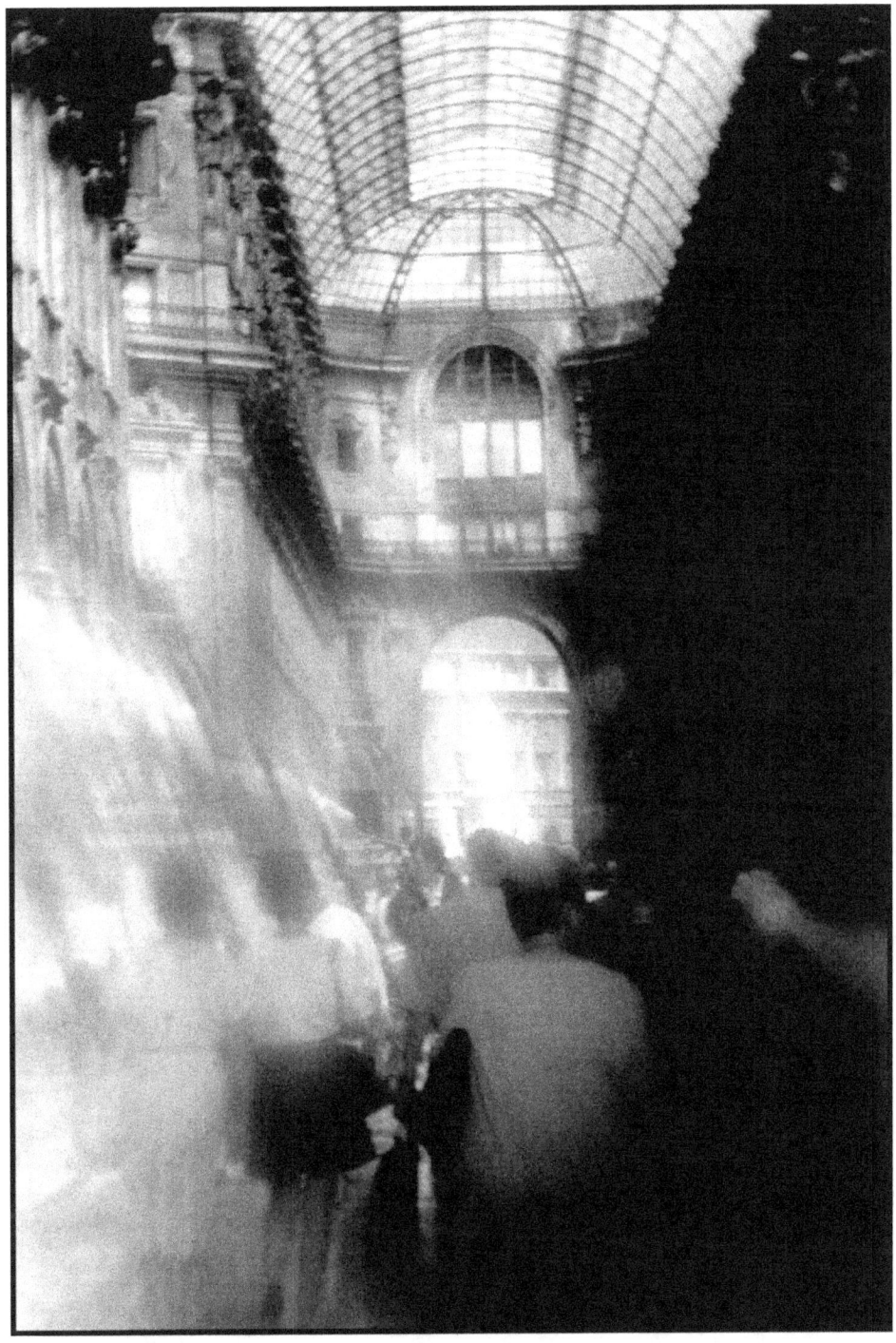

1971 - Milan – V. Emanuele Gallery - Yashica FX3 - Ilford Pan F - Devel. Microfen

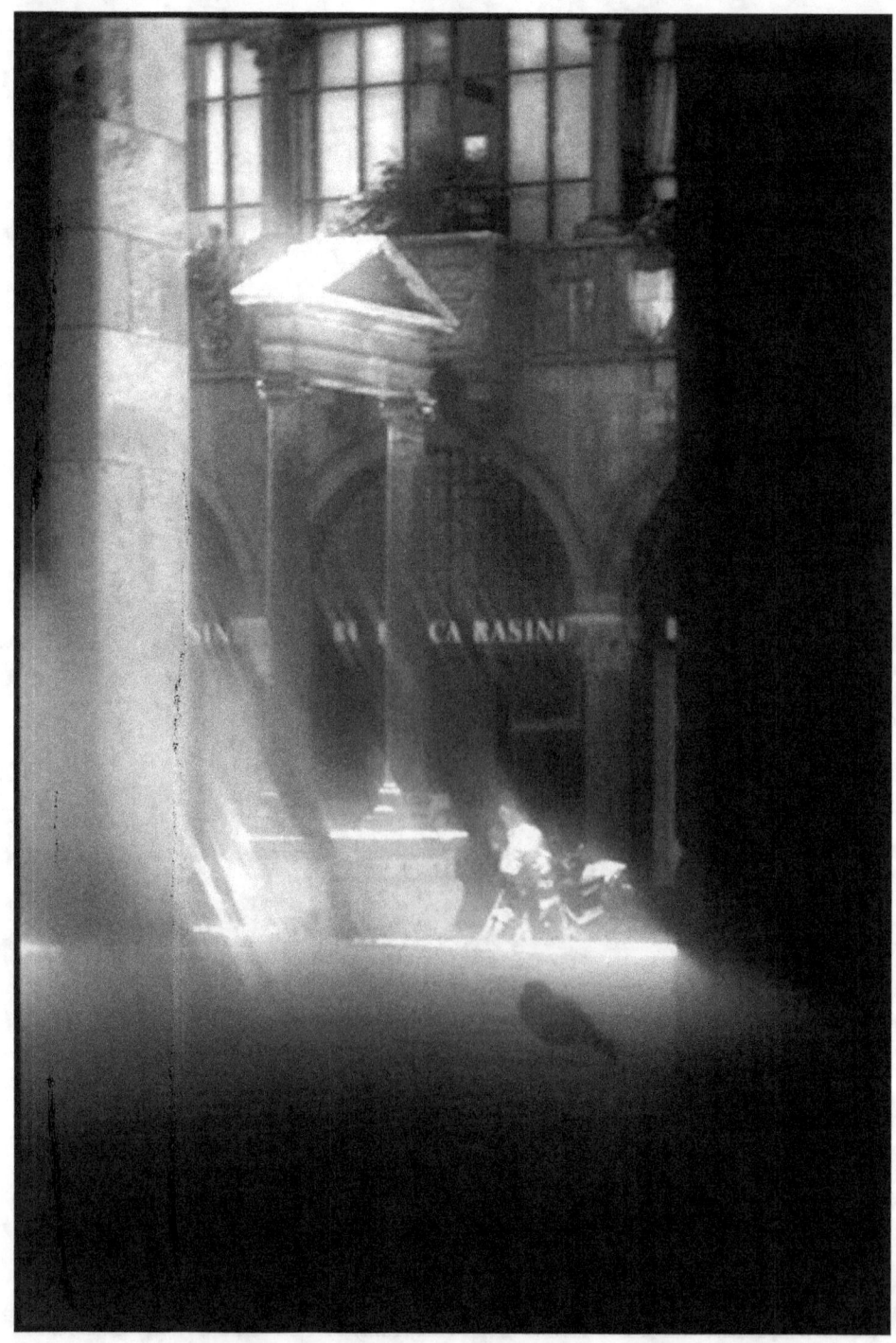

1971 - Milan - Piazza Mercanti - Yashica FX3 - Ilford Pan F - Devel. Microfen

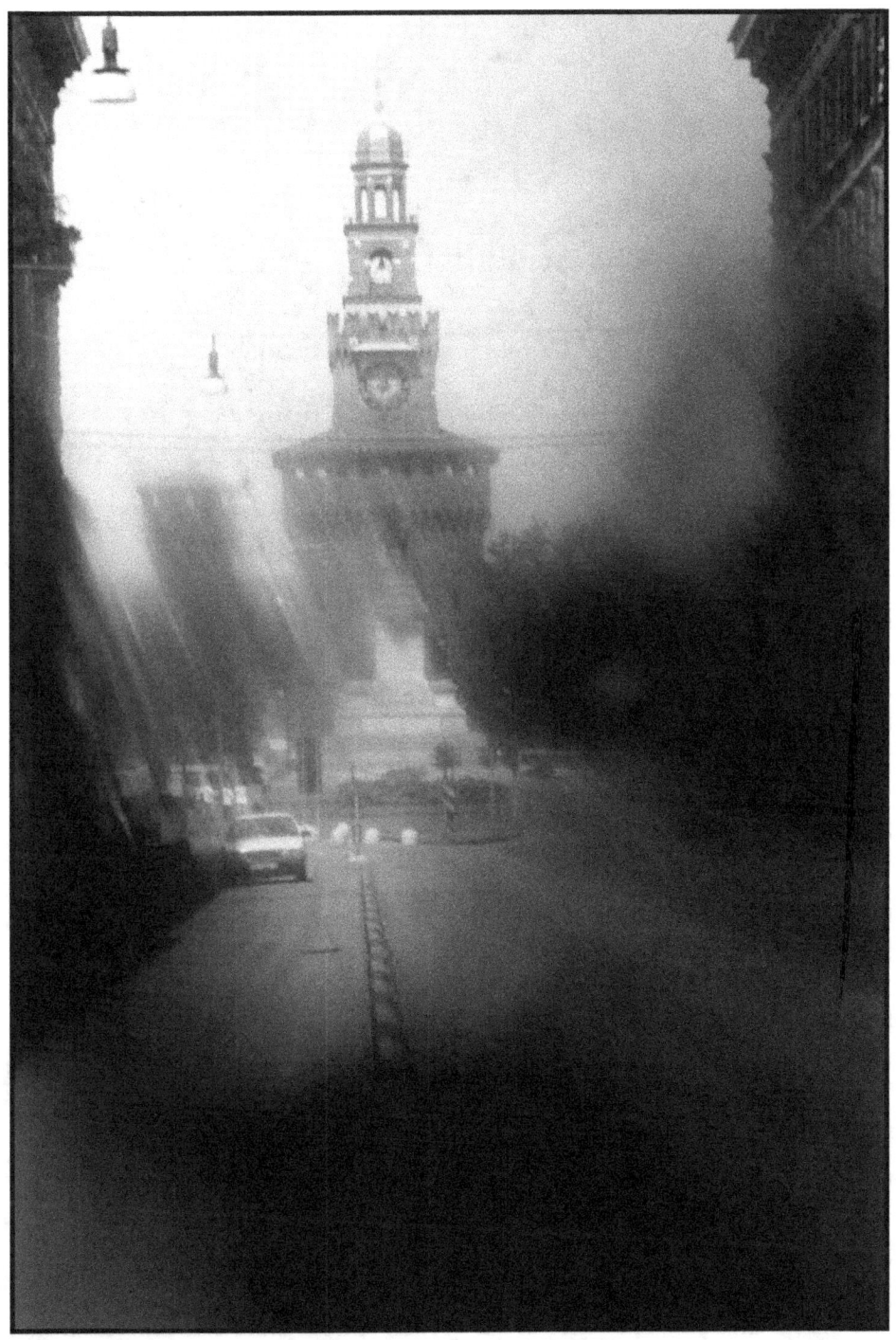

1971 - Milan – Sforza Castel - Yashica FX3 - Ilford PAN F - Devel. Microfen

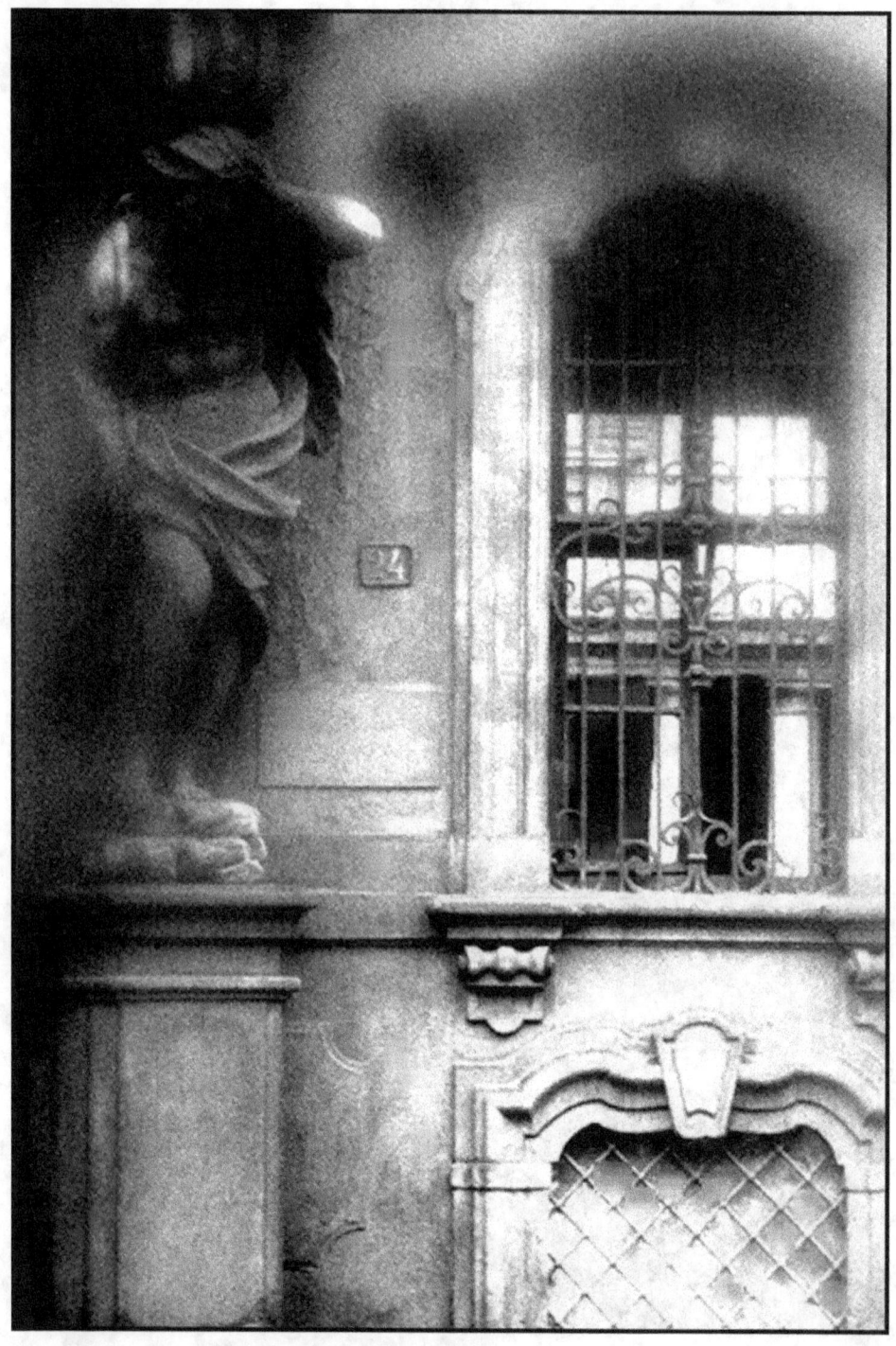

1971 - Milan – Omenoni Palace- Yashica FX3 - Ilford PAN F - Devel. Kodak D76

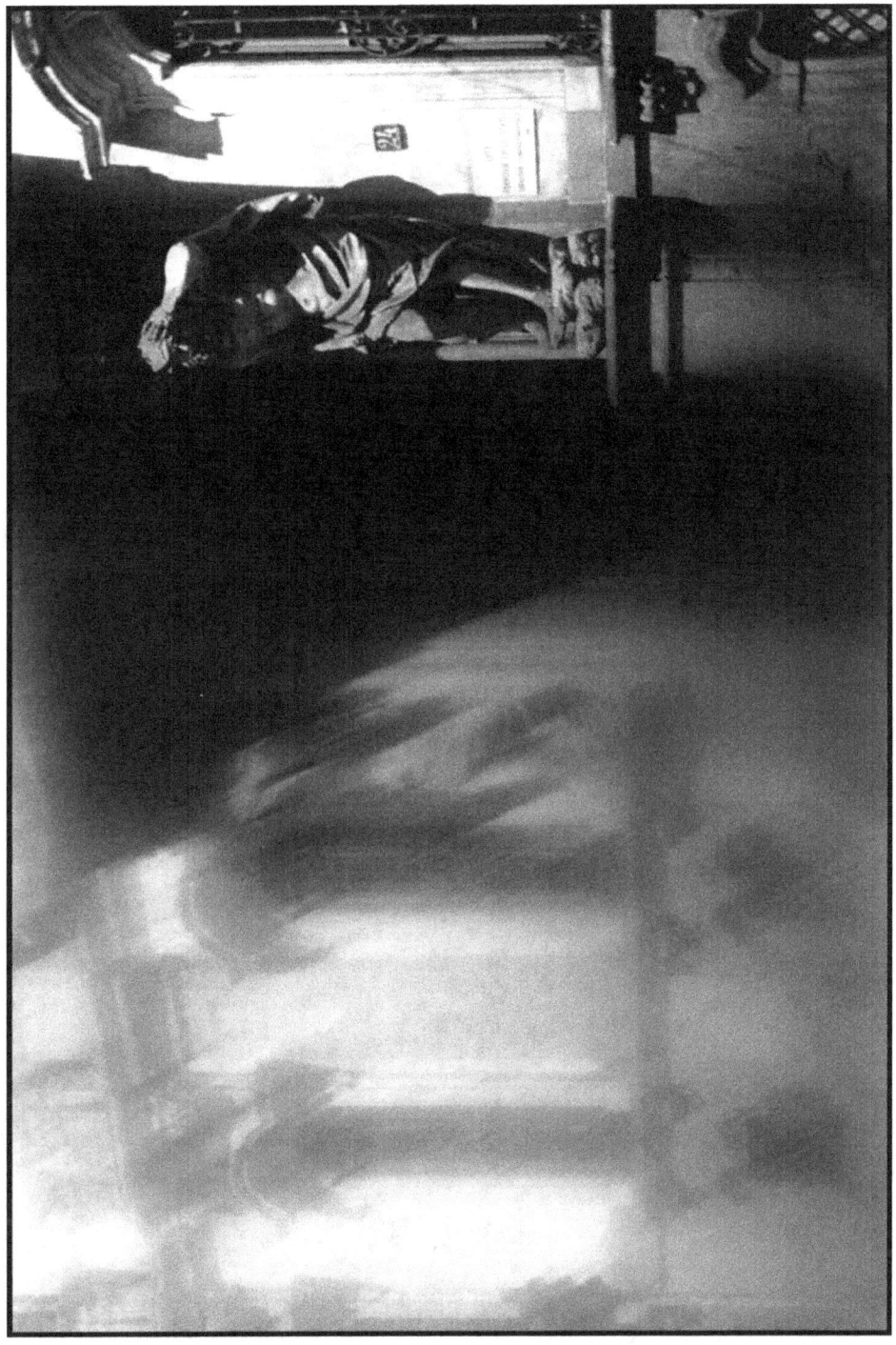

1978 - Milano – Omenoni Palace - Yashica FX3 - Ilford FP4 - Sviluppo. Microfen

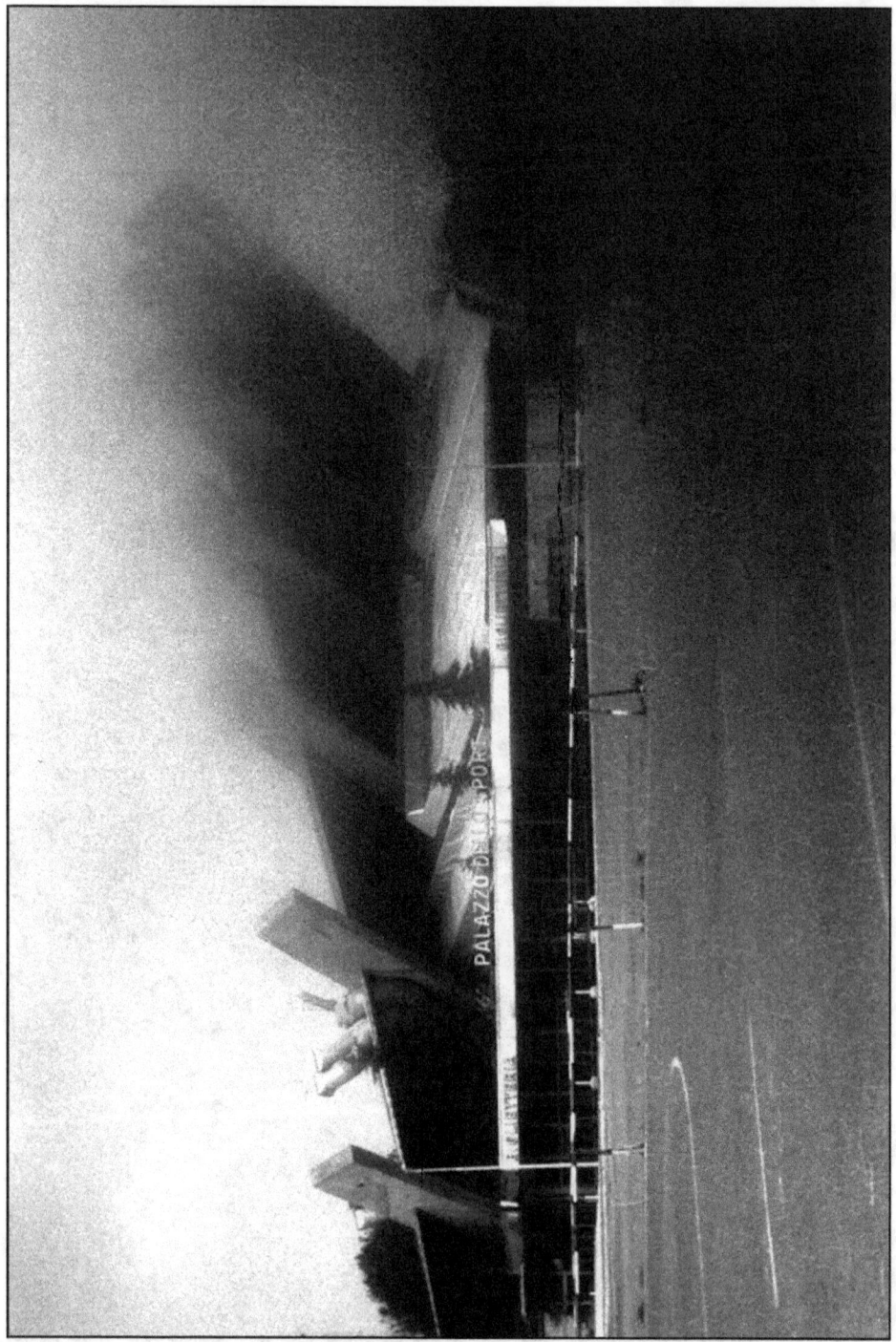

1982 - Milan – Vigorelli Velodrome - Yashica FX3 - Ilford FP4 - Devel. Microfen

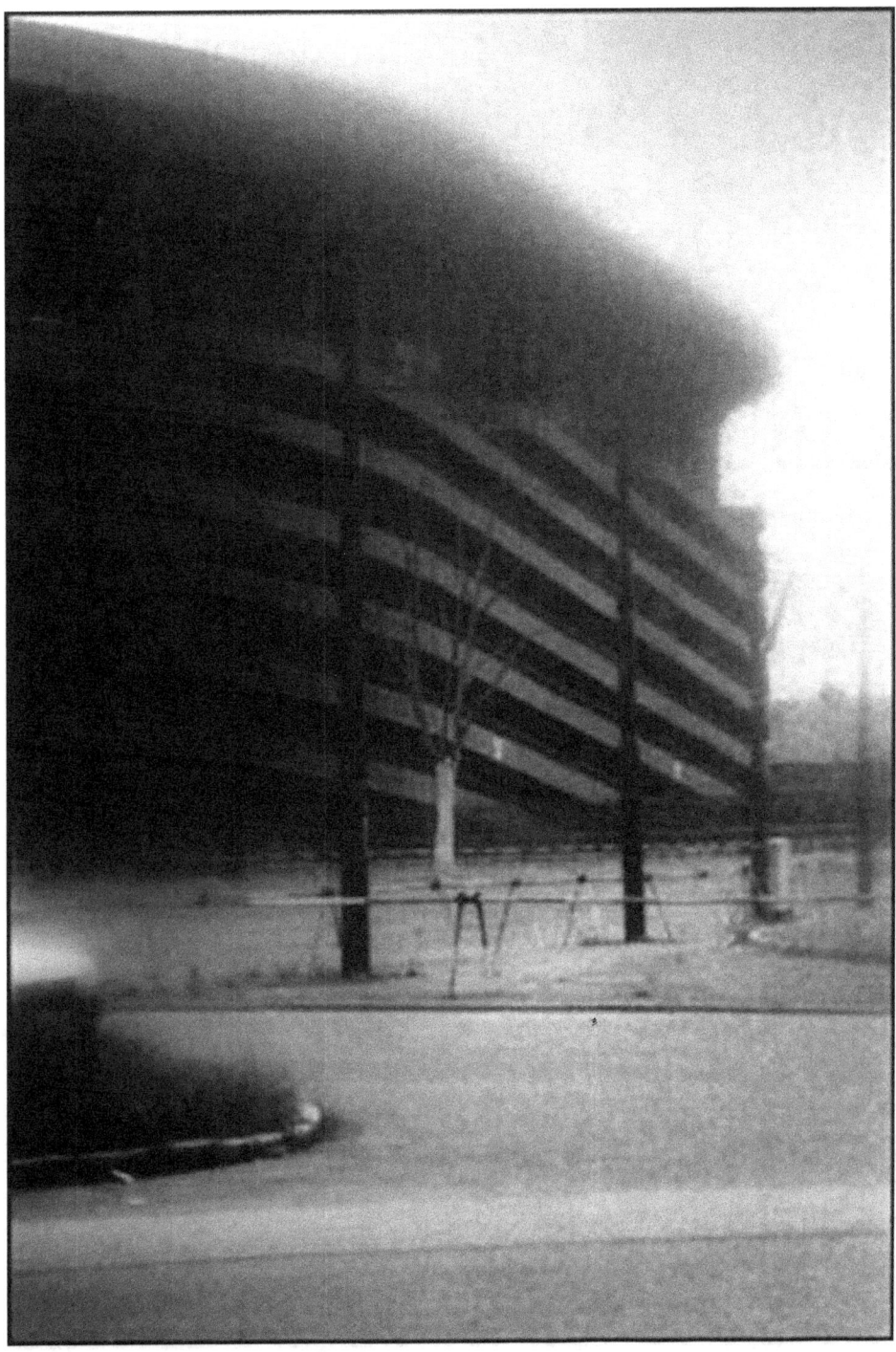

1978 - Milan – Old San Siro stadium - Yashica FX3 - Ilford FP4 - Devel. Microfen

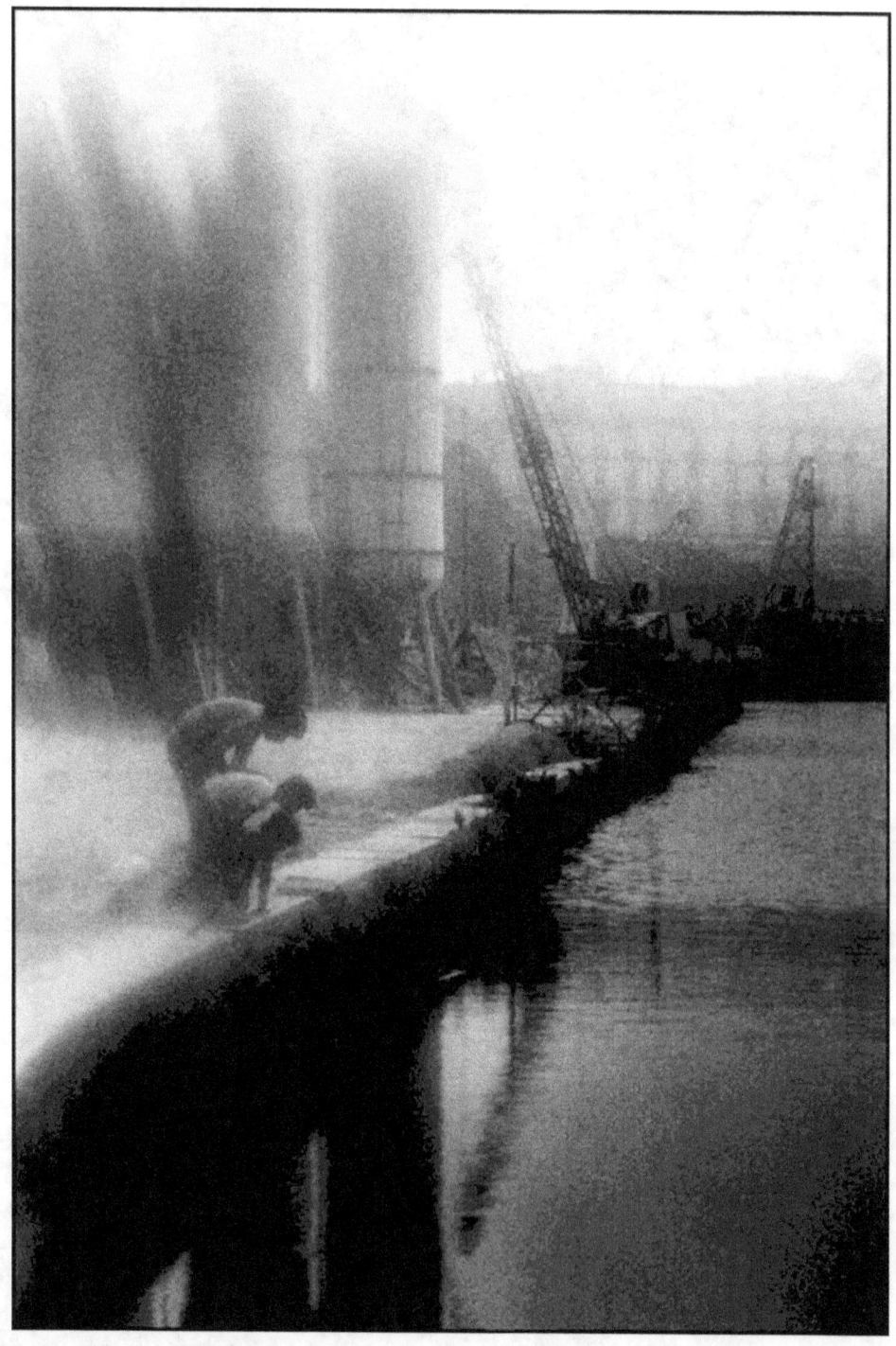

1982 - Milan – The dock - Yashica FX3 - Agfapan 400 - Devel. Microfen

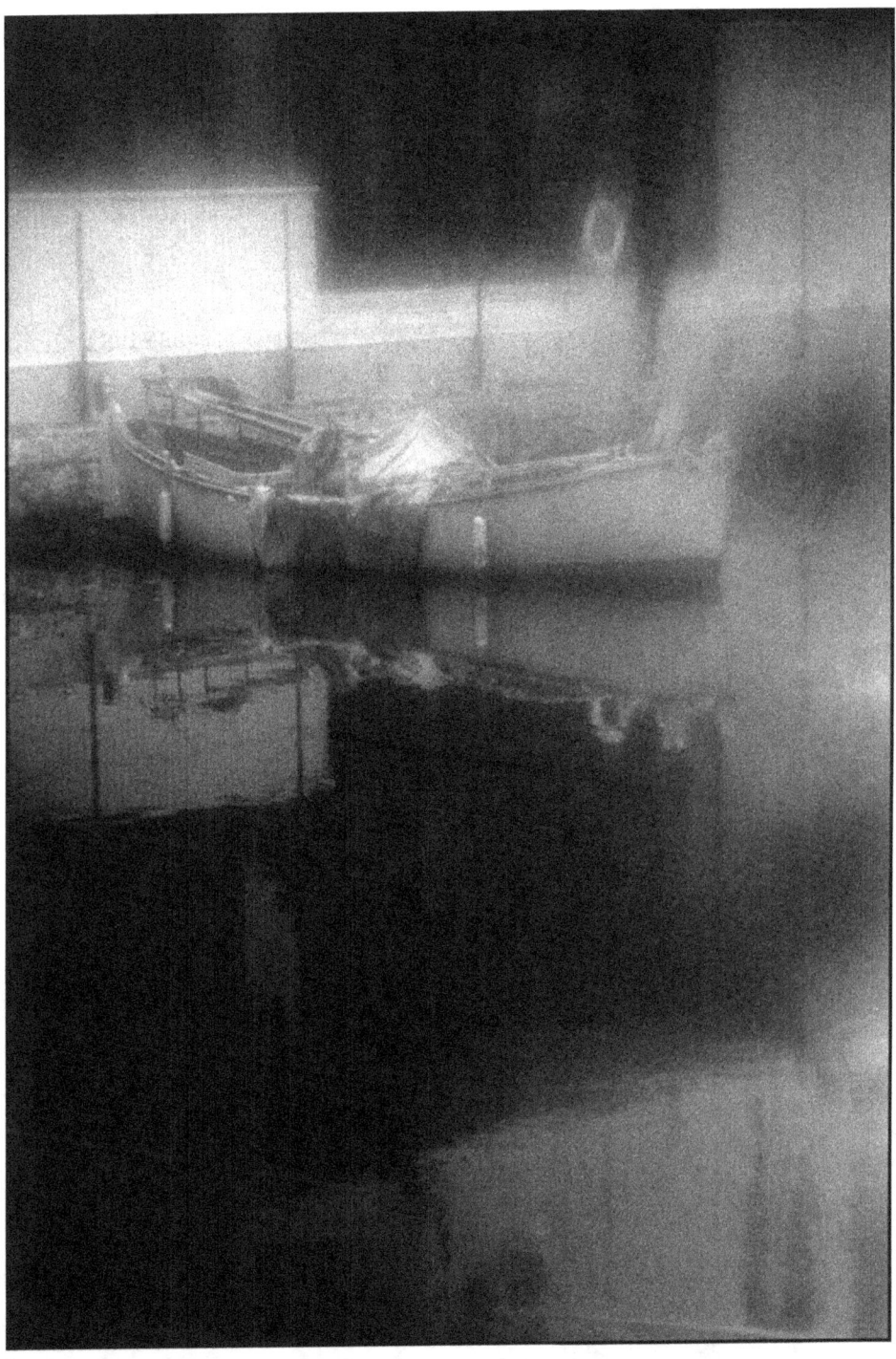

1982 - Milan – Boat on the canal - Yashica FX3 - AgfaPan 400 - Devel. Microfen

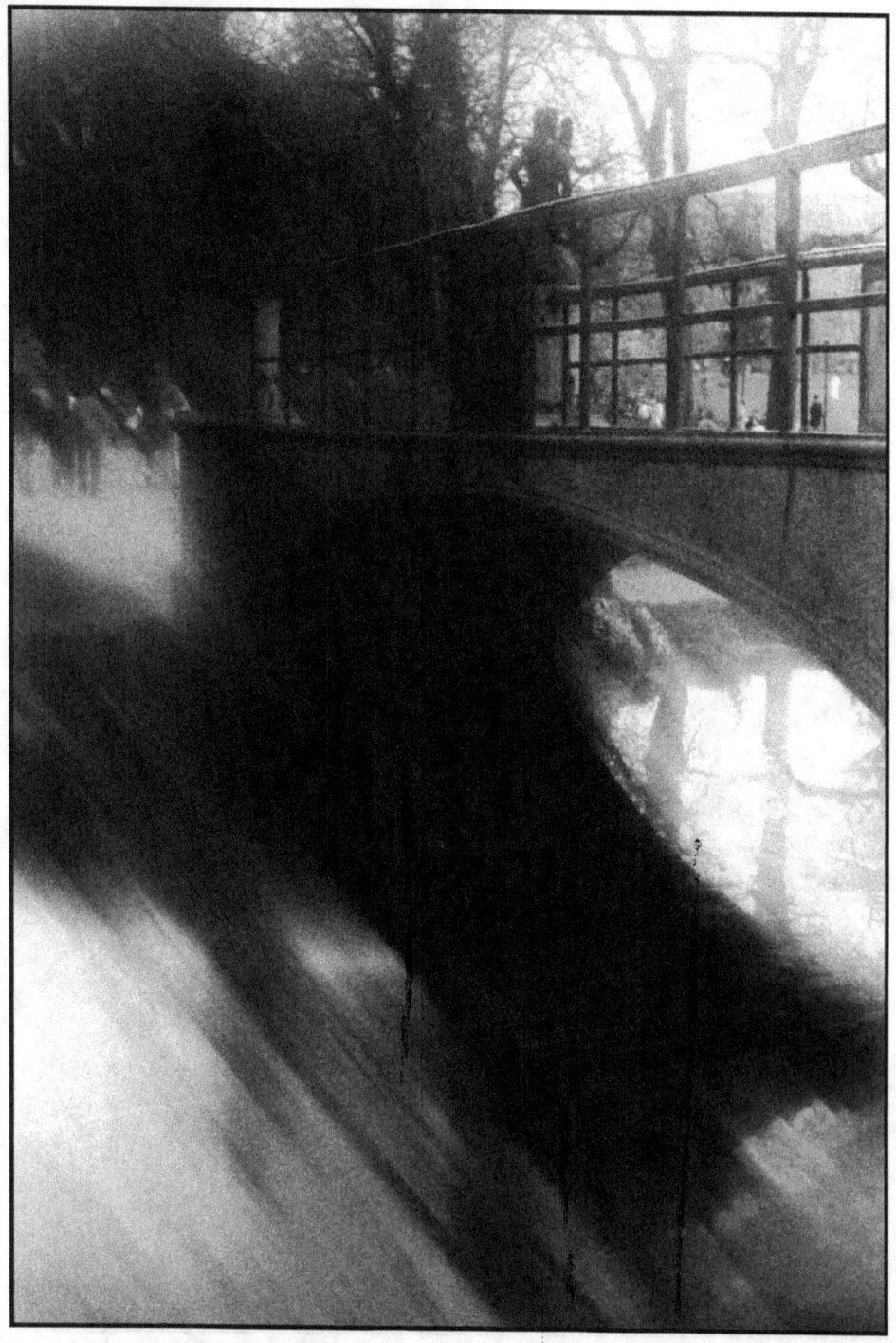

1982 - Milan – Little mermaid bridge - Olympus OM2 - Ilford FP4 - Devel. D76

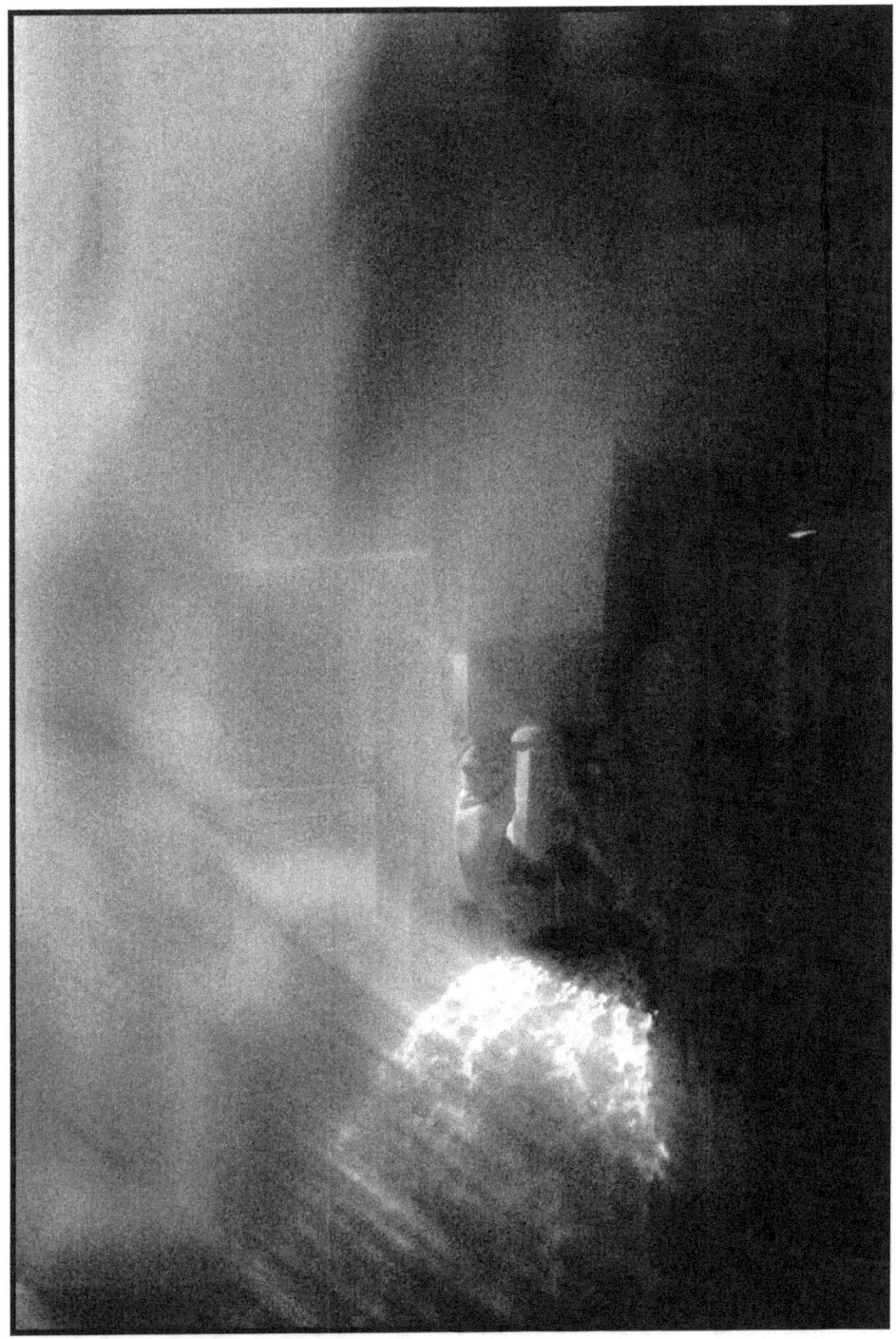

1978 – Milan - Central station - Olympus OM1 - PAN F - Devel. Microfen

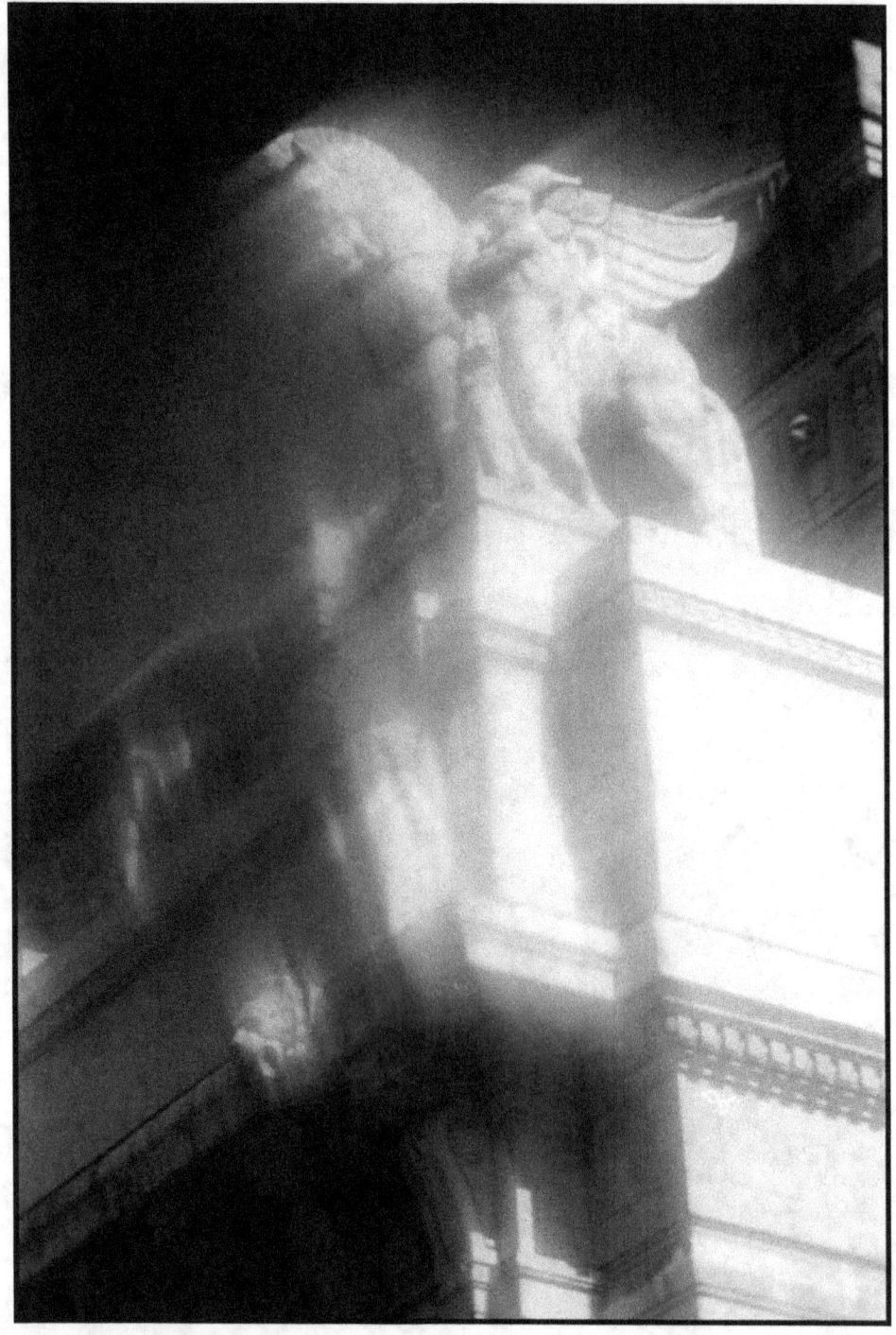

1971 - Milan – Central station - Yashica FX3 - Ilford PAN F - Devel. Microfen

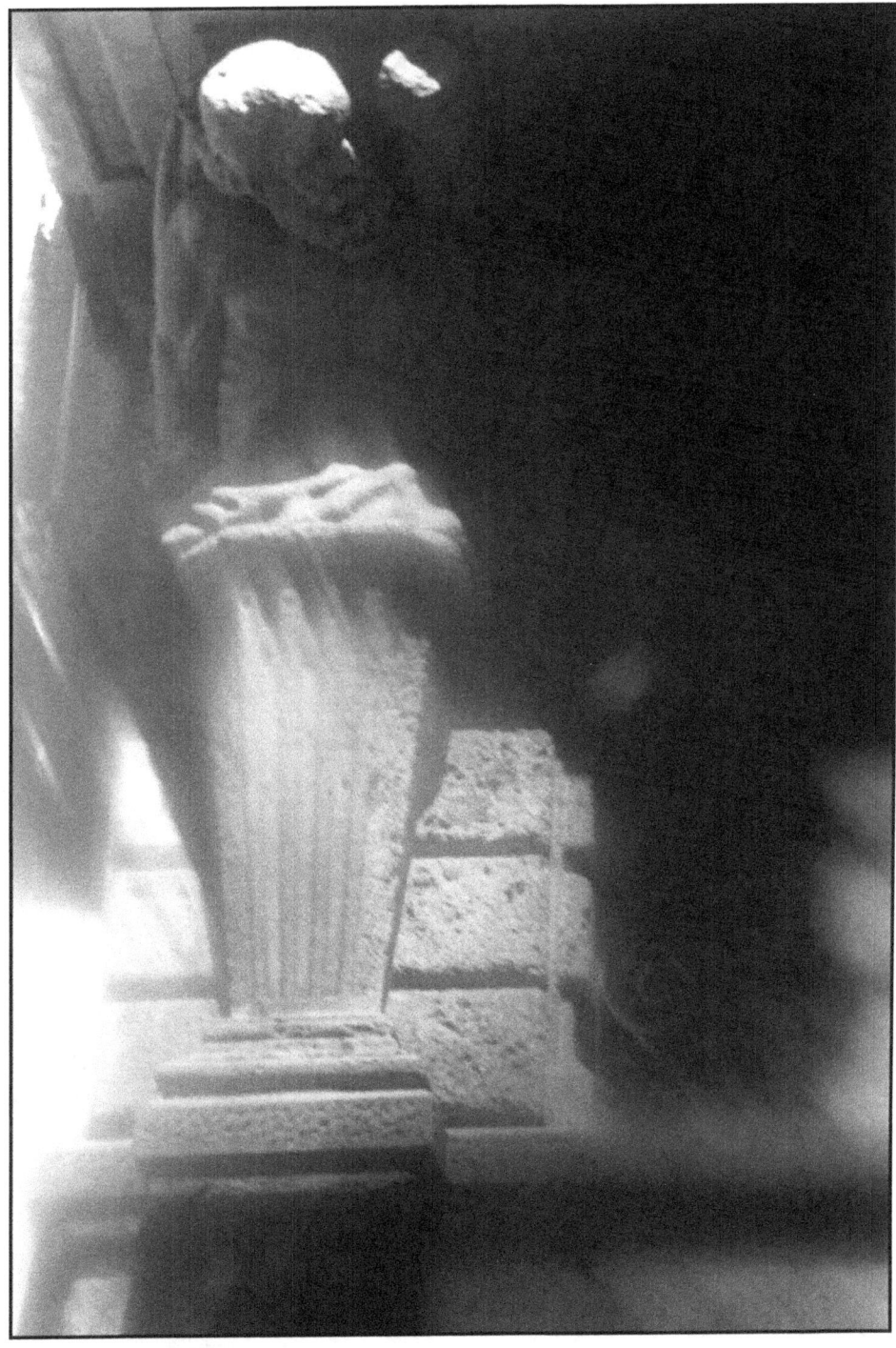

1971 - Milan – Boccaccio Street - Yashica FX3 - Ilford PAN F - Devel. Microfen

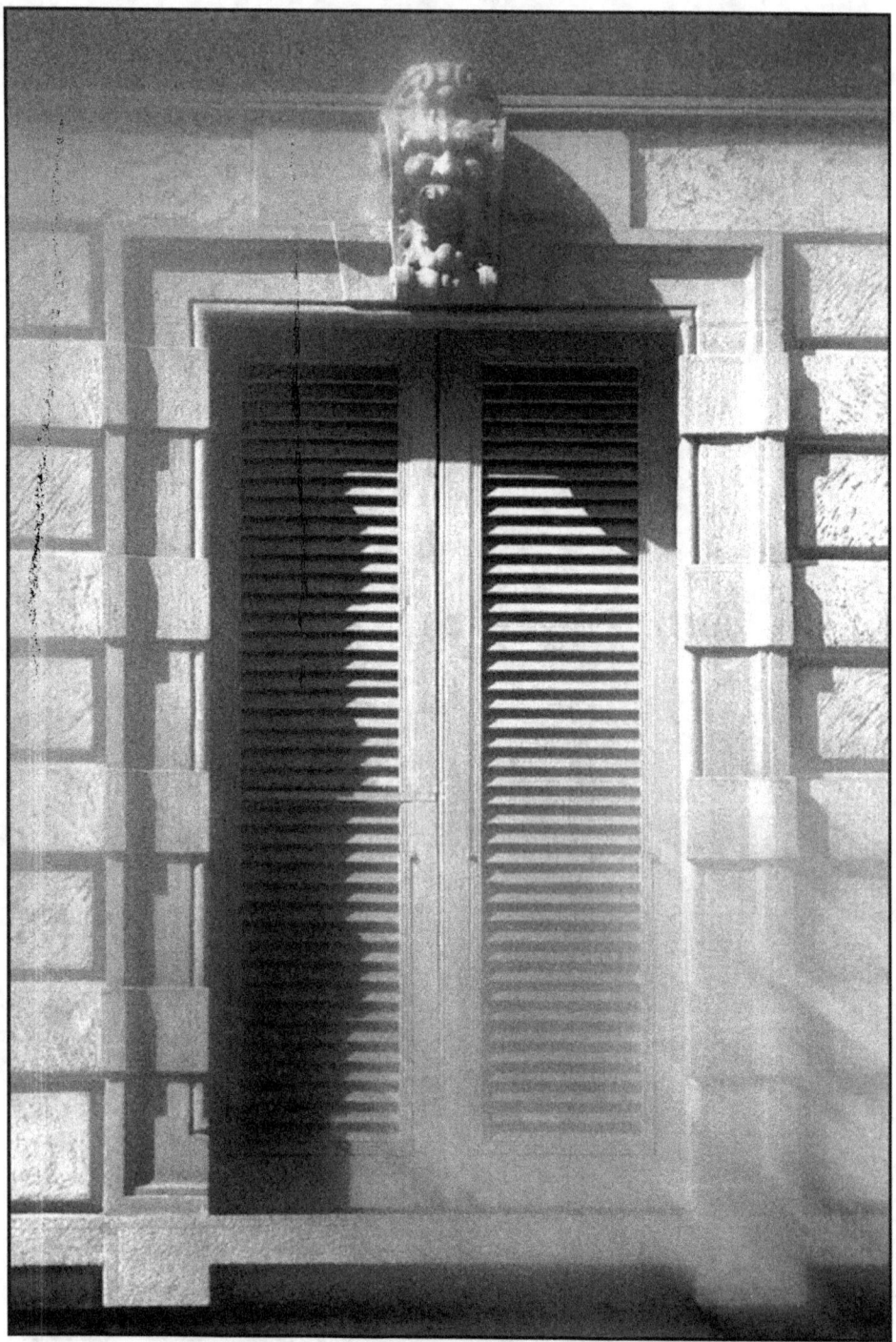

1971 - Milan – Boccaccio Street - Yashica FX3 - Ilford PAN F - Devel. Microfen

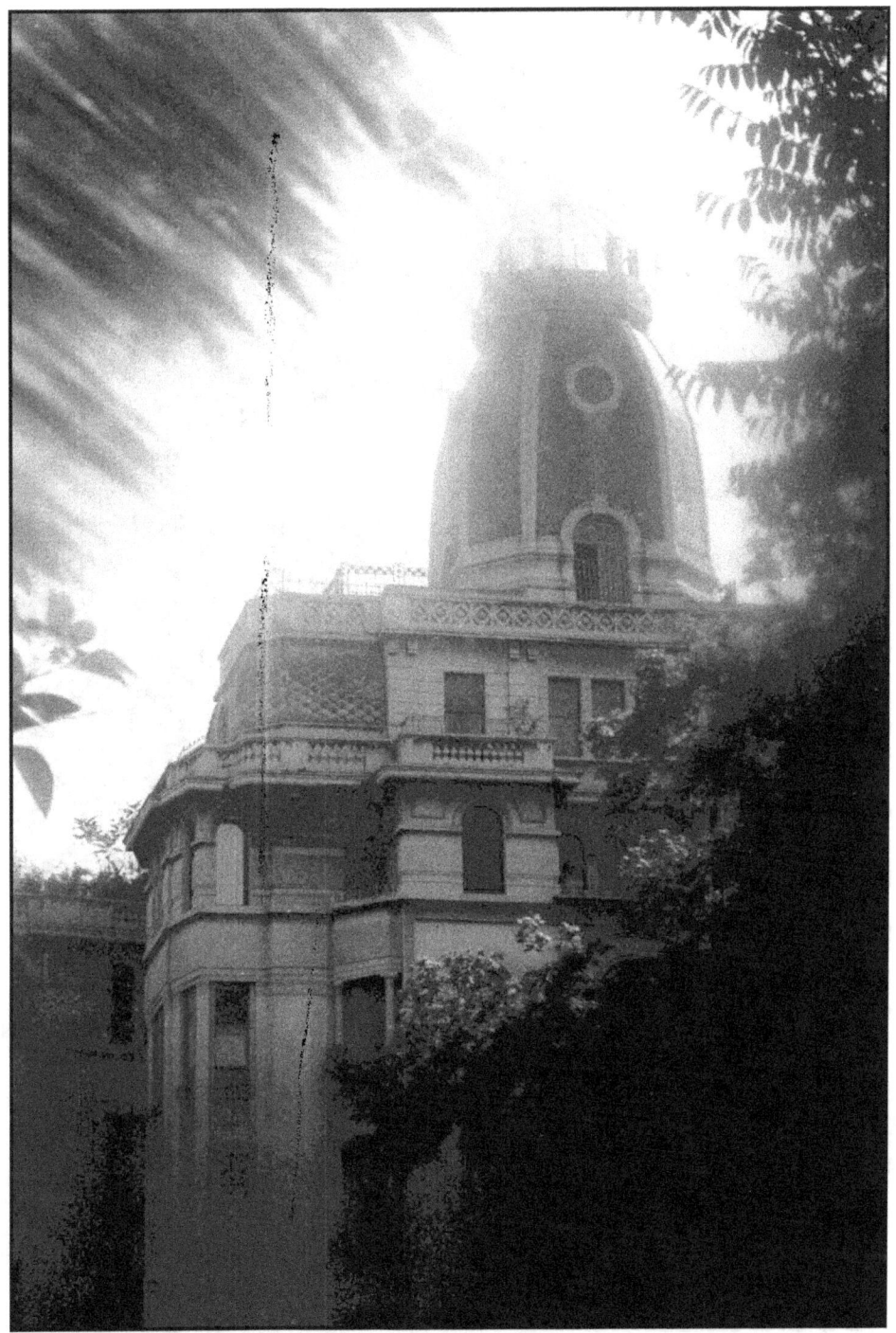

1971 - Milan – Piemonte Square - Yashica FX3 - Ilford PAN F - Devel. Microfen

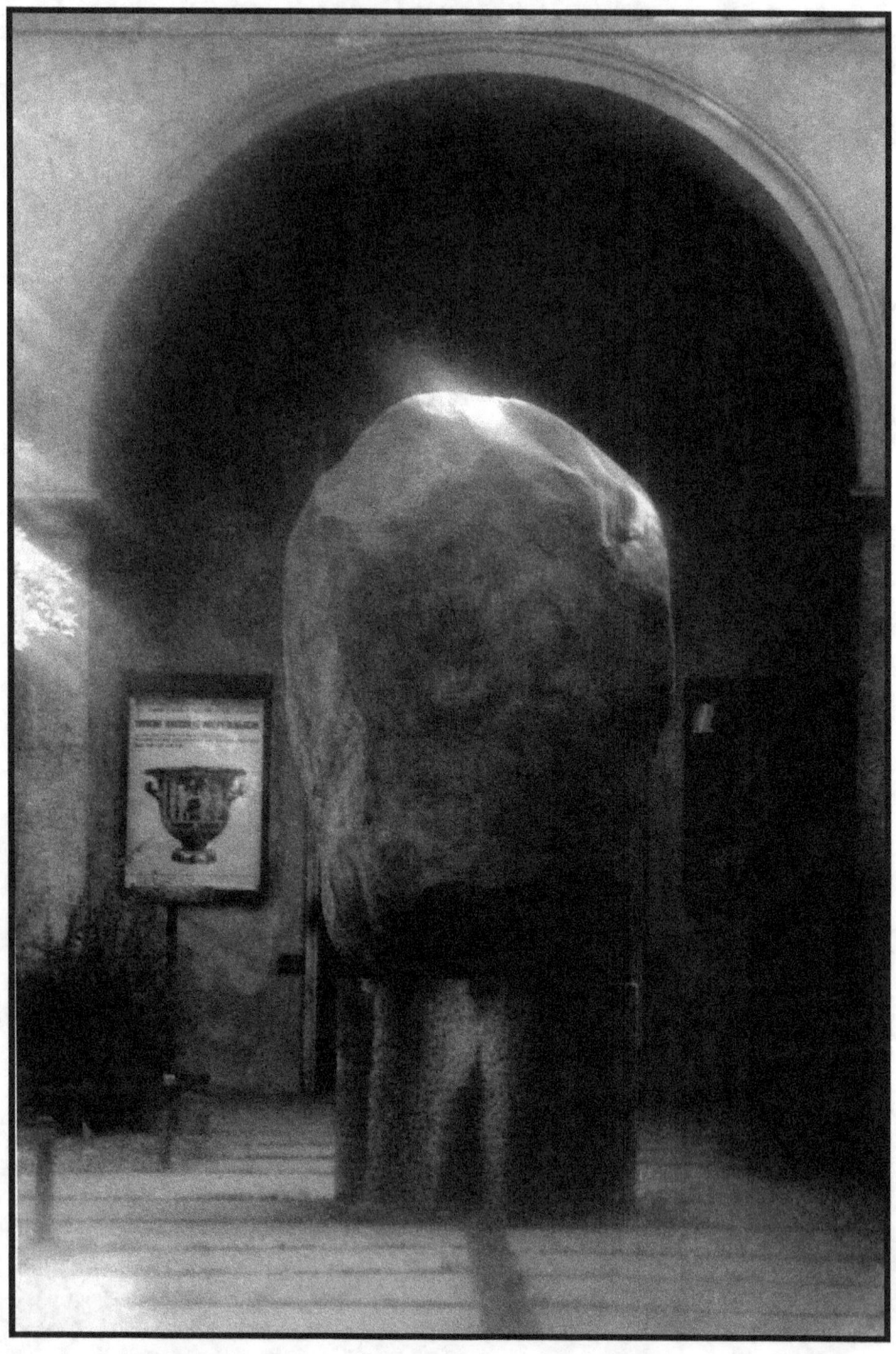

1980 – - Milan – Archeological Museum - Yashica FX3 - Ilford PAN F - Devel. Microfen

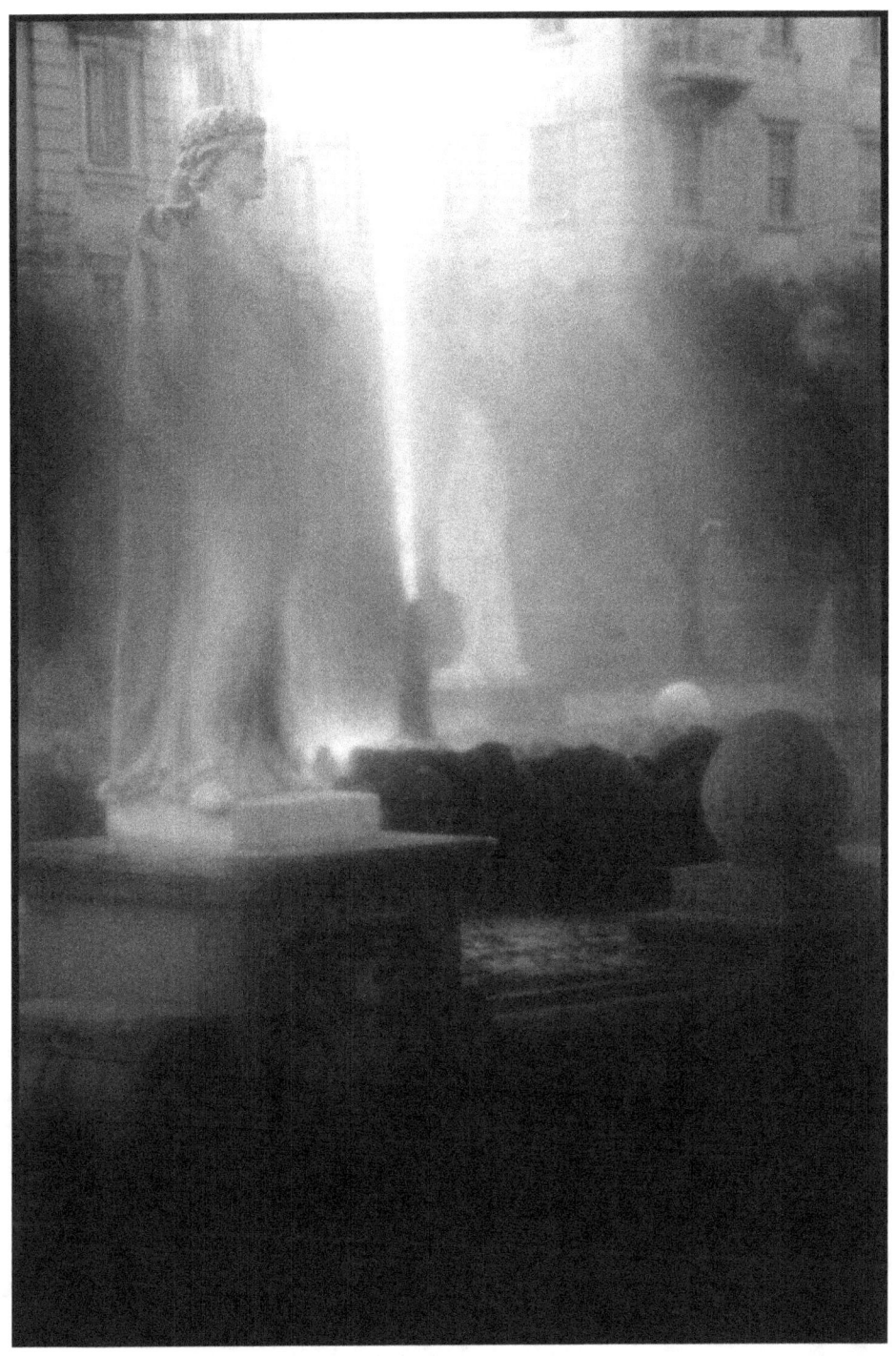

1978 – Milan - Fountain - Olympus OM1 - Ilford PAN F - Devel. Microfen

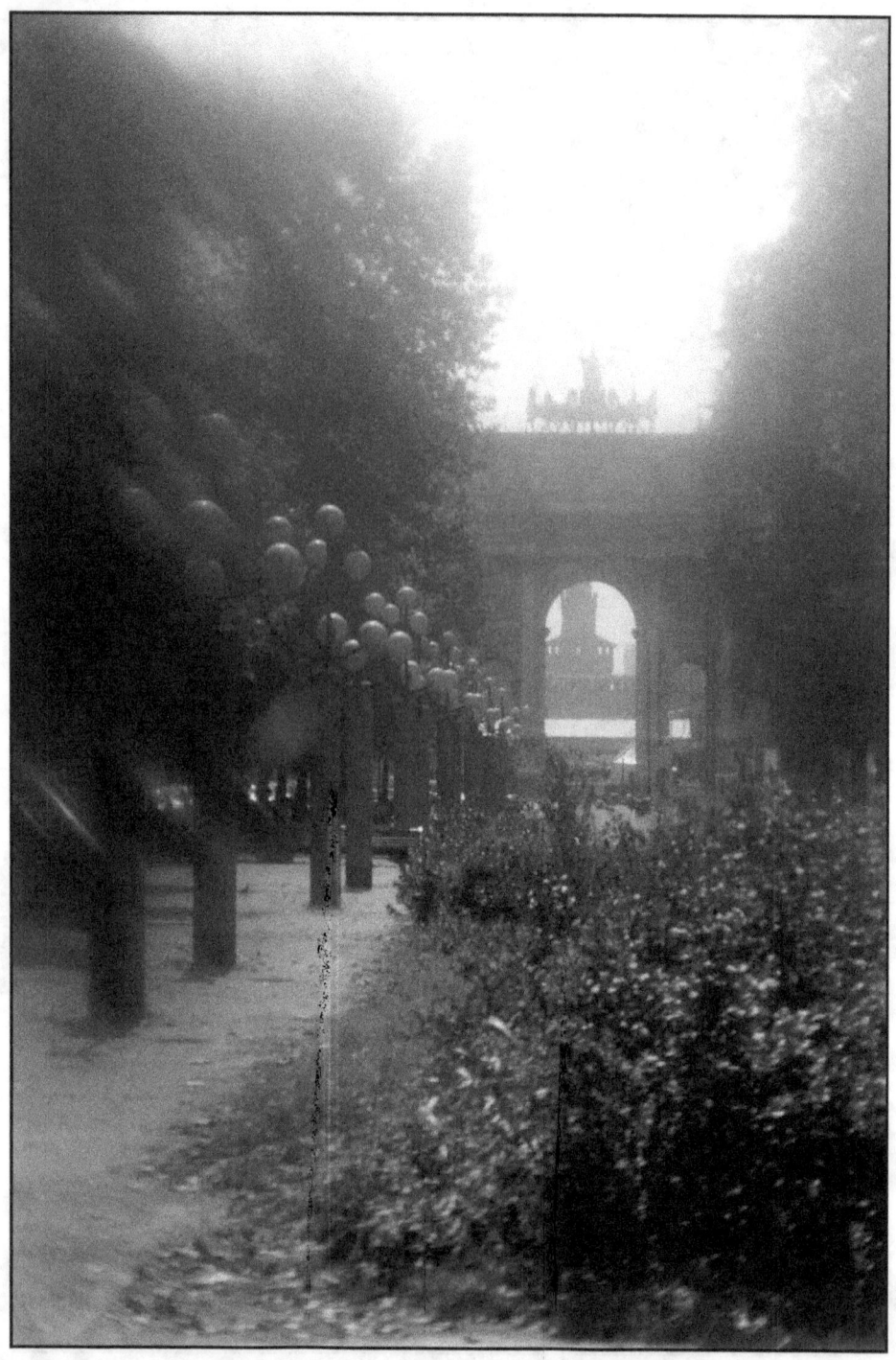

1971 - Milan – Triumph Arch - Yashica FX3 - Ilford PAN F - Devel. Microfen

FOTOART

*

FOTOART

3 RURAL CIVILISATION OF SOUTHERN ITALY

Faces engraved by time, happiness for small essential things, abandoned houses, importance of seemingly useless things, are the obvious result of a land tormented by a thousand existential problems, a thousand situations and conditions.

This Calabrian land of which I am a son, that has nourished me between blinded suns and miseries, this Calabrian land, I said, that has always filled me with deep sensory perceptions and that has bound me to the universal simplicity of its people, has been able to give me the strength of feeling, the impetuosity of love and the appreciation of humility.

In a world of violence, of excessive sensations, of the unheard-of search for the pleasures of the moment and not of the whole of existence, it has often been a refuge of thought, cradle of ancient feelings, richness of creative images.

FOTOART

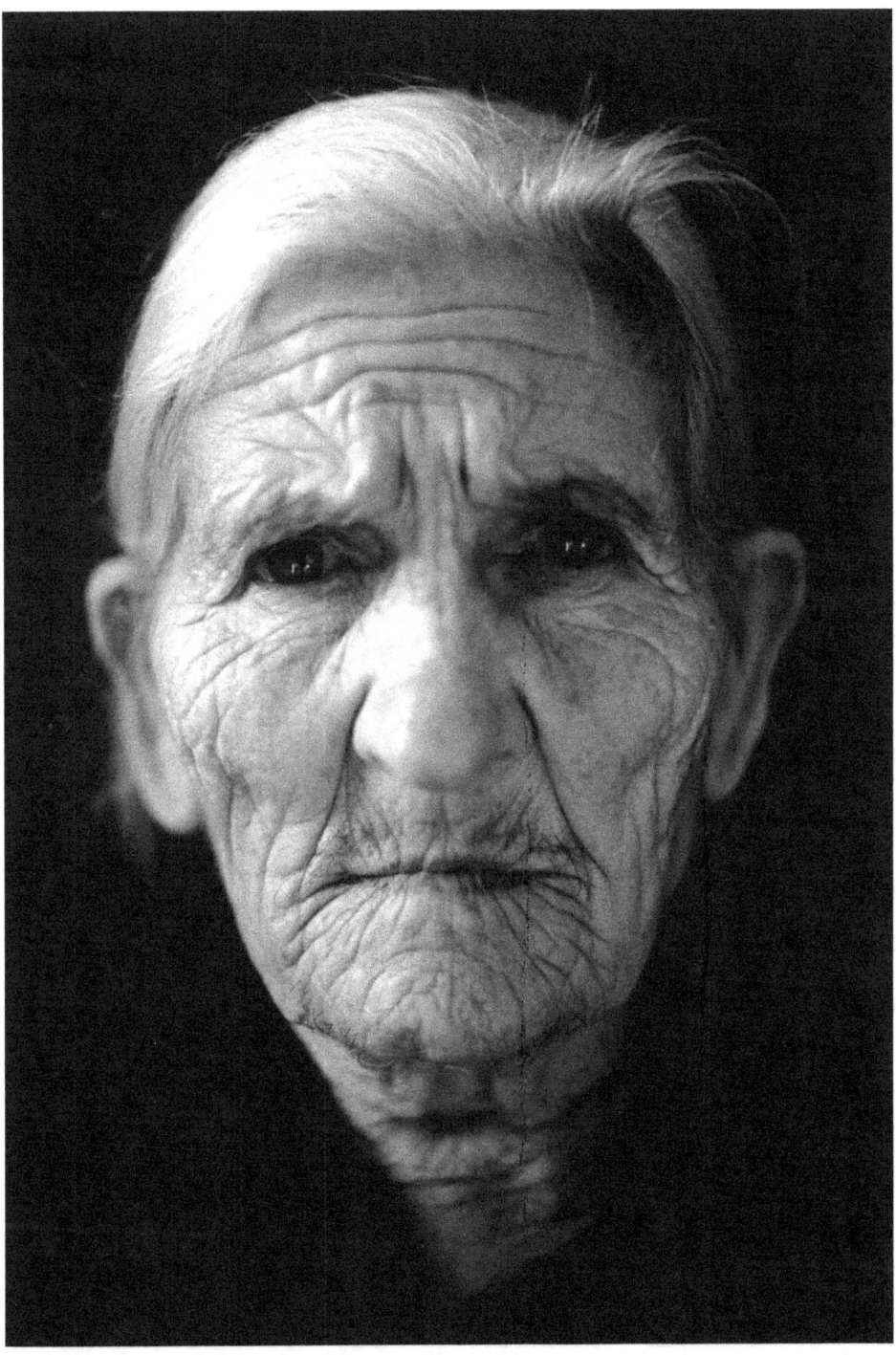

1978 – Limpidi (VV) - Calabrian woman - Koroll 35 - Ferrania P3 – Devel. Rodinal.

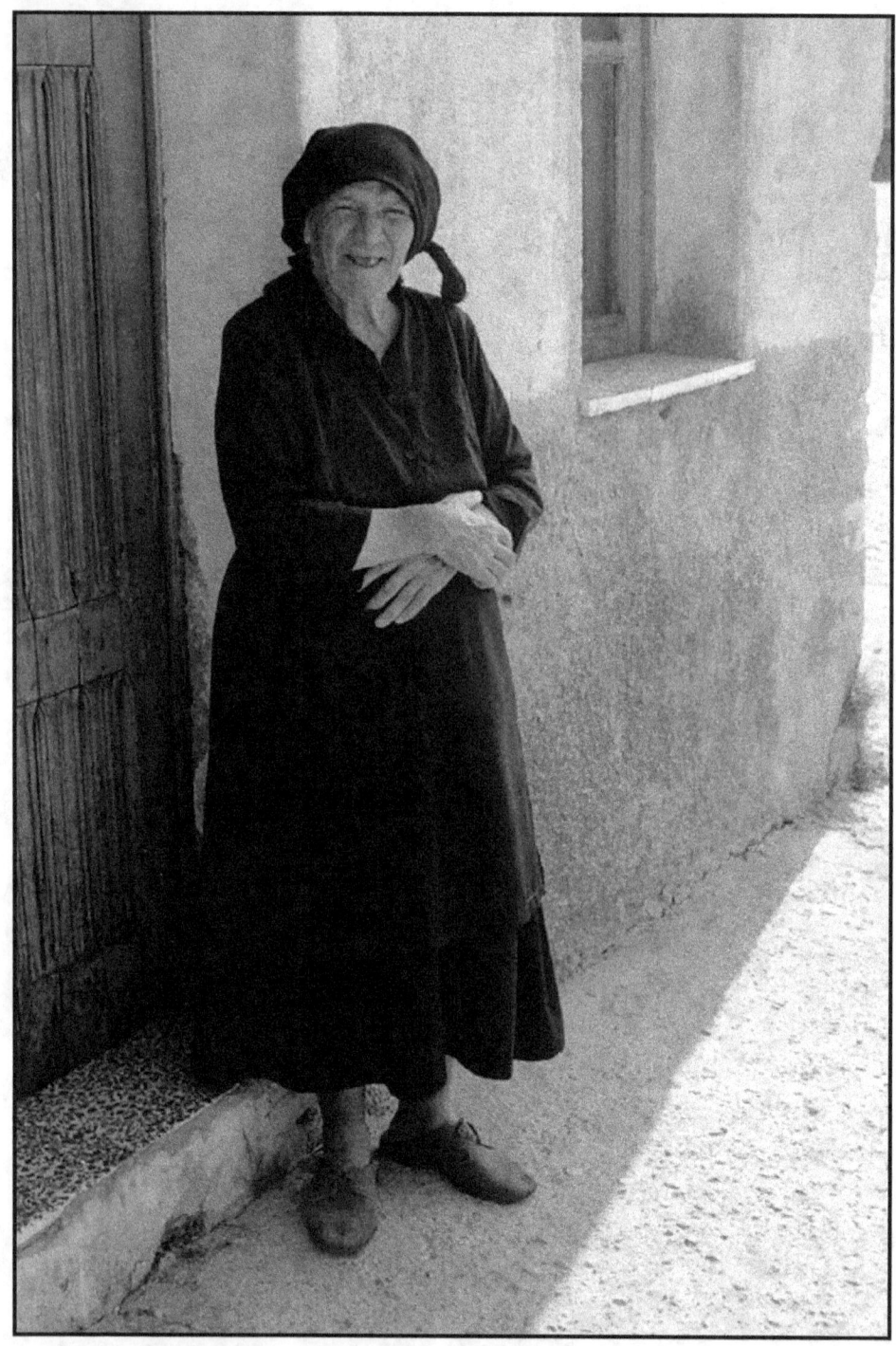

1978 - Zungri (VV) - Calabrian woman - Koroll 35 - Ferrania P3 – Devel. Rodinal

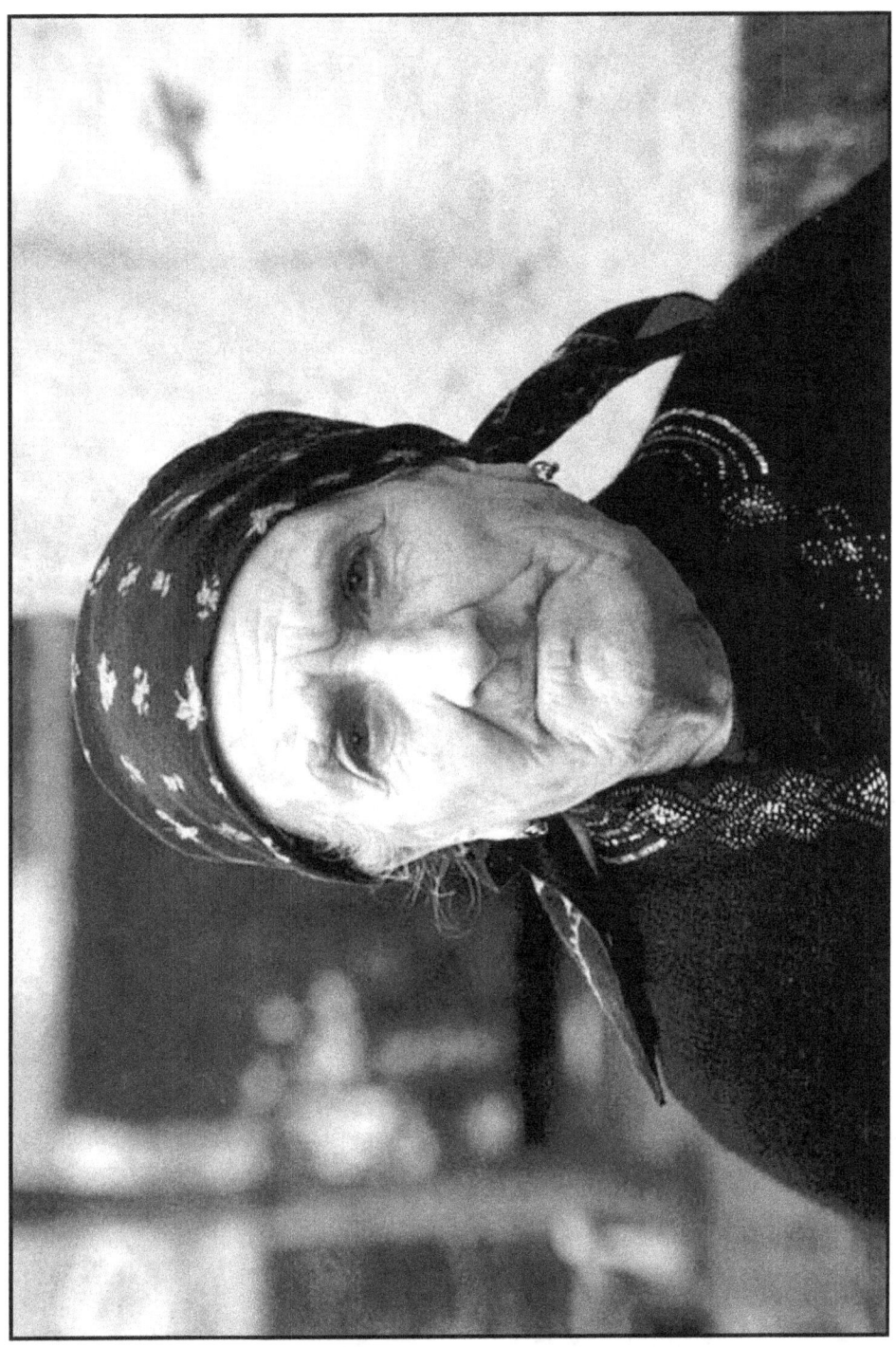

1977 - Limpidi (VV) – Calabrian woman - Minolta XD - FP4 - Devel. D76

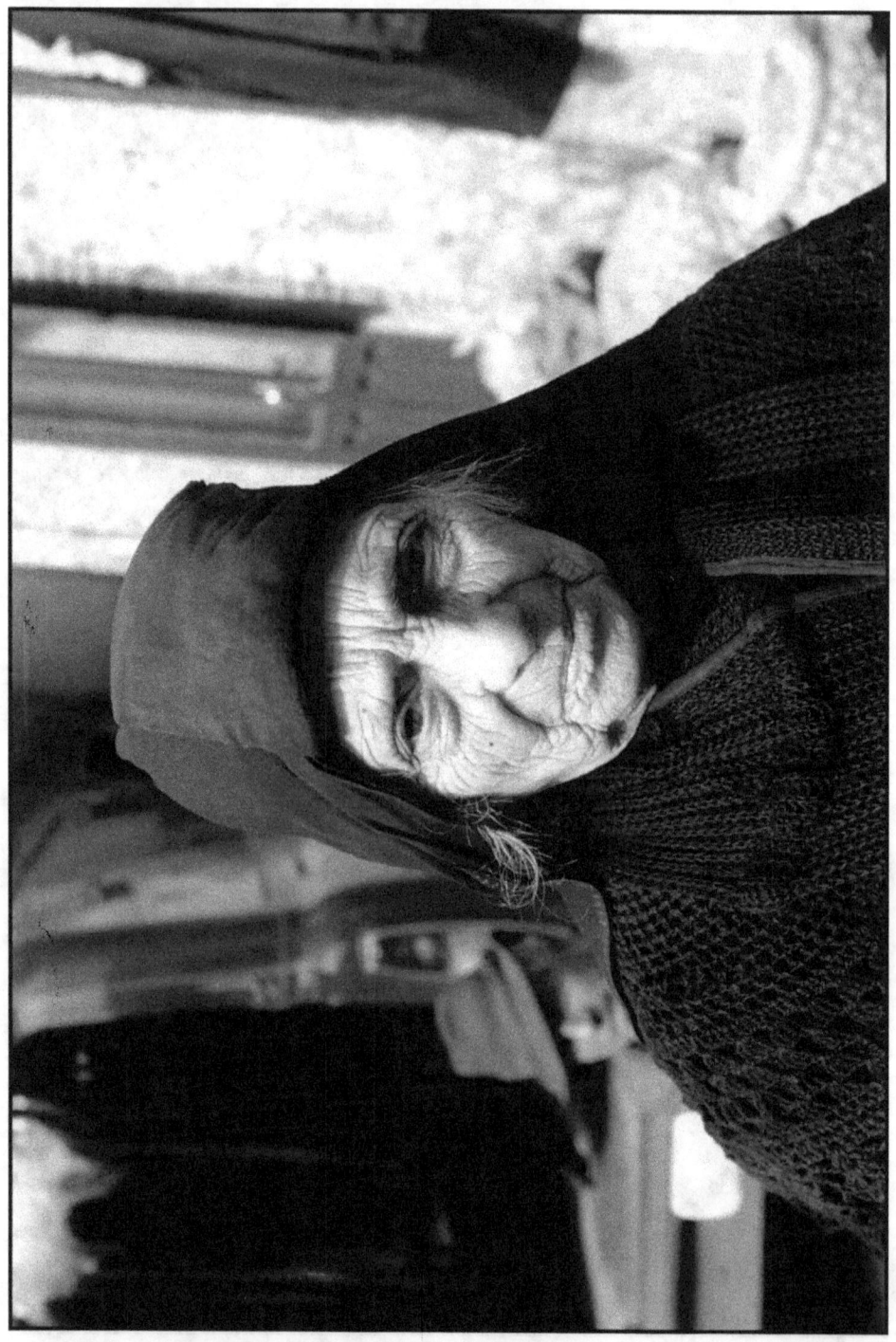

1978 - Soriano (VV) - Calabrian woman - Koroll 35 - Ferrania P3 – Devel. Rodinal

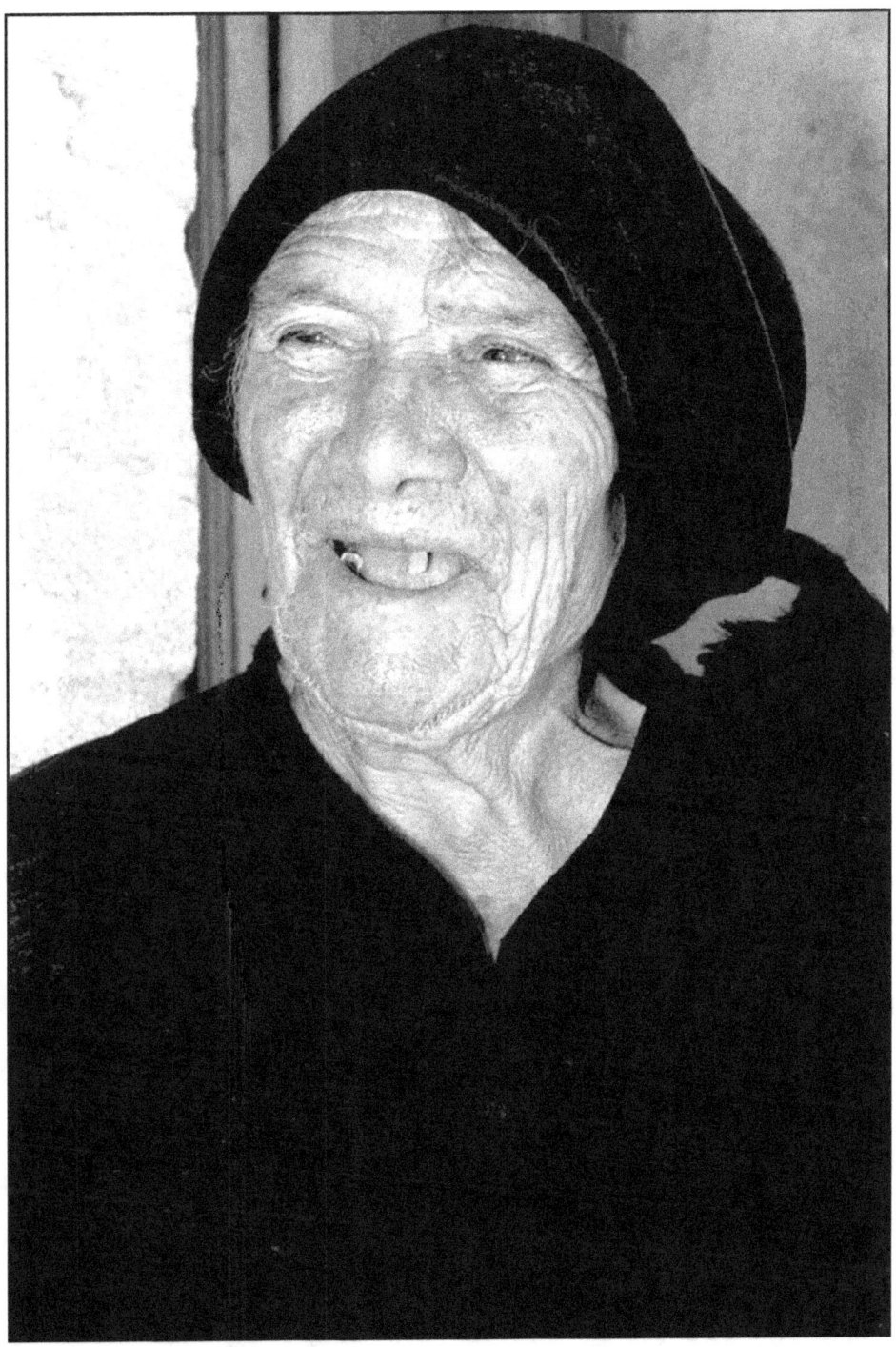

1977 - Soriano (VV) – Calabrian woman - Minolta XD - FP4 - Devel. D7

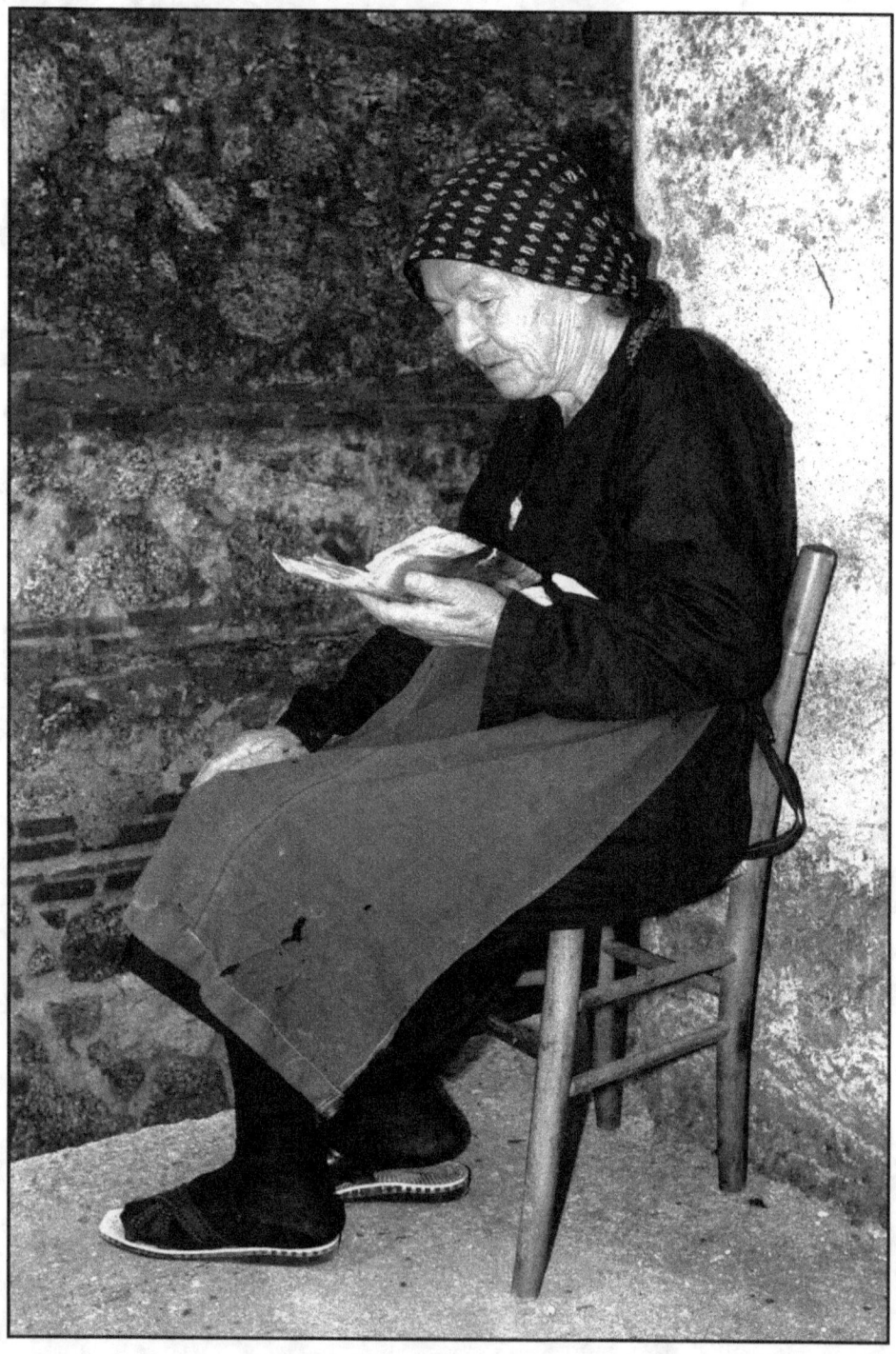
1977 – Seminara (RC) – Calabrian woman - Minolta XD - FP4 - Devel. D76

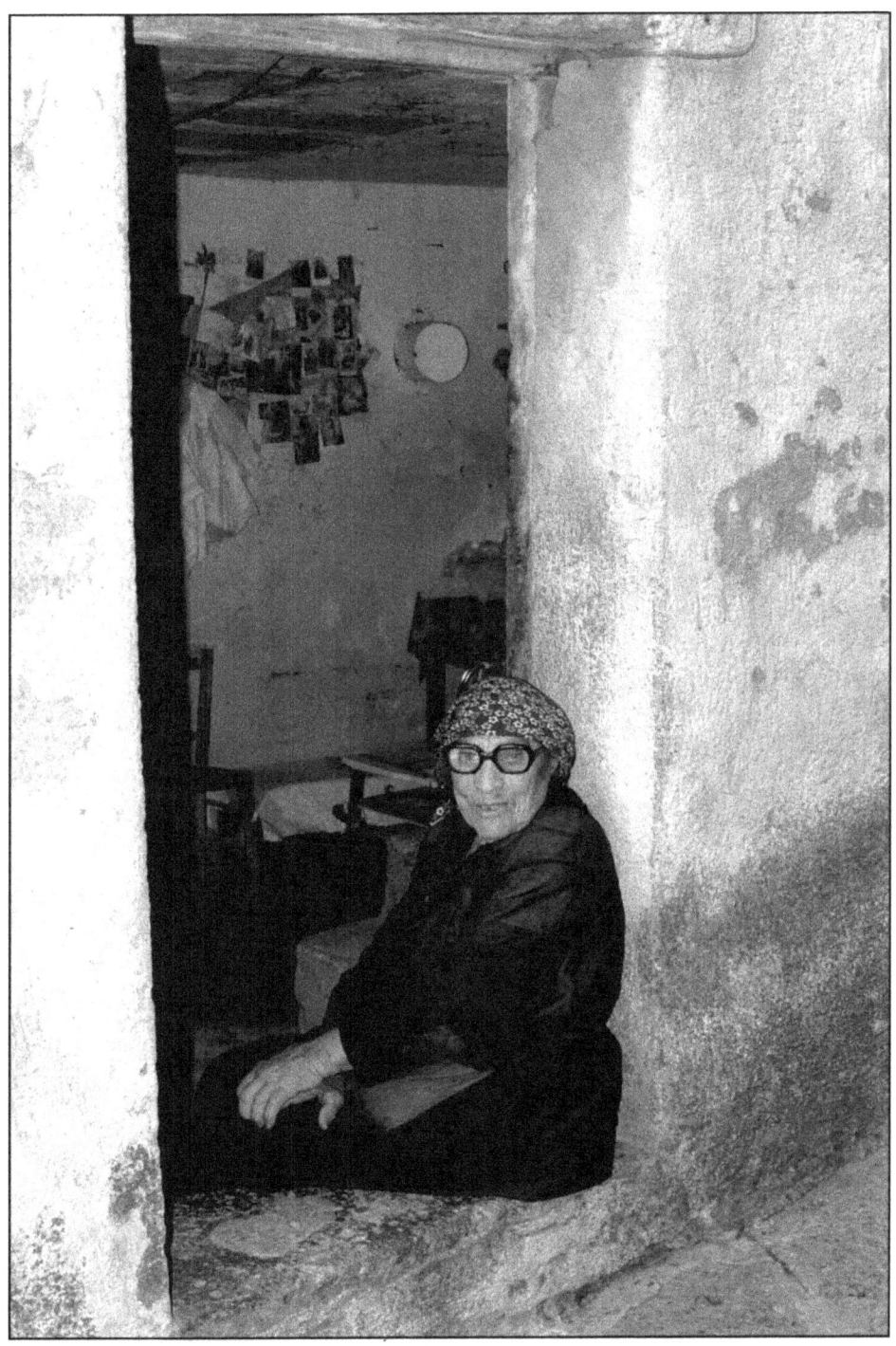

1977 - Soriano (VV) – Calabrian woman - Minolta XD - FP4 – Devel. D76

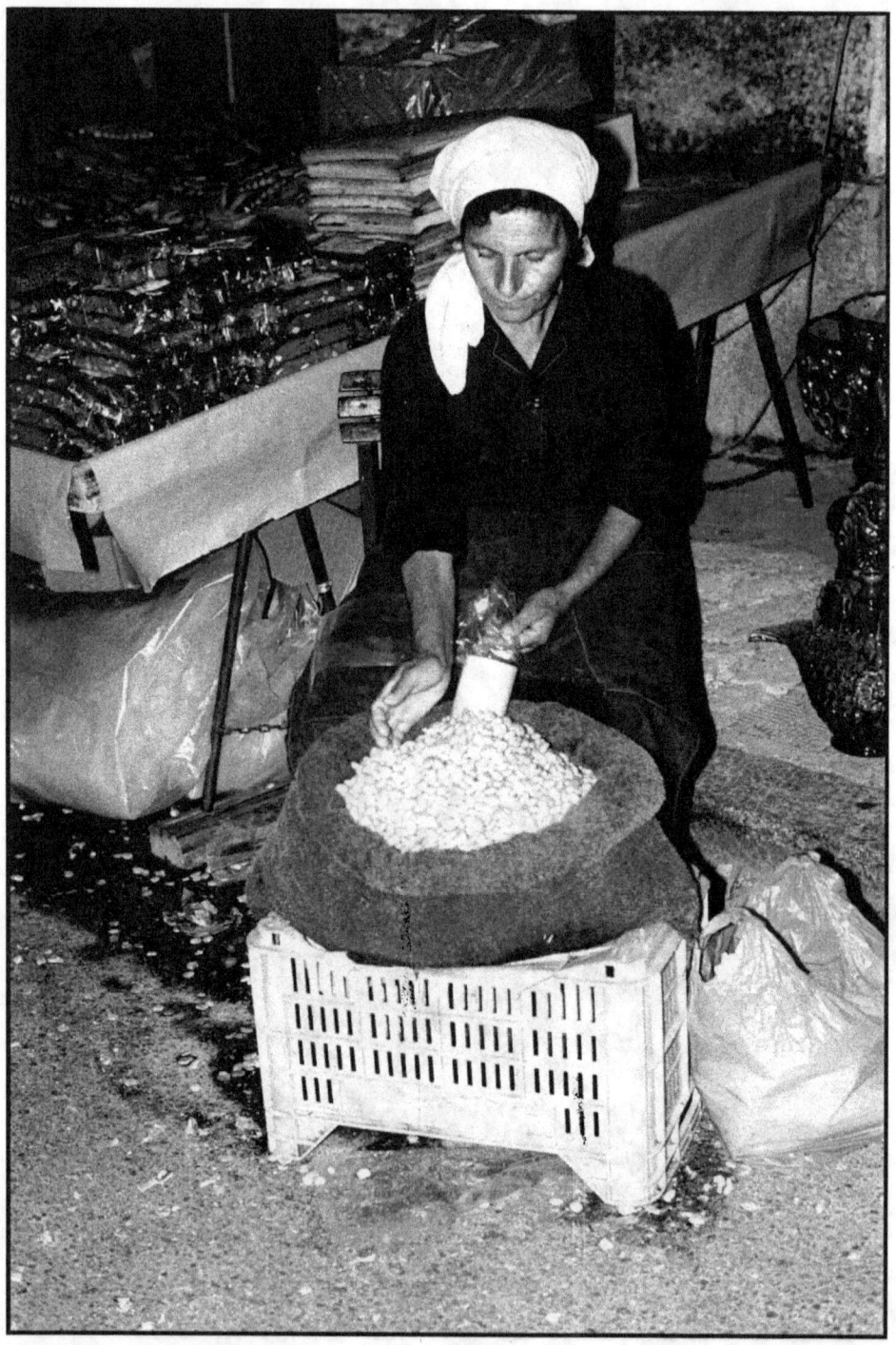

1978 – S. Calogero (VV) - Lupine seller – Koroll 35 - Ferrania P3 – Devel. Rodinal

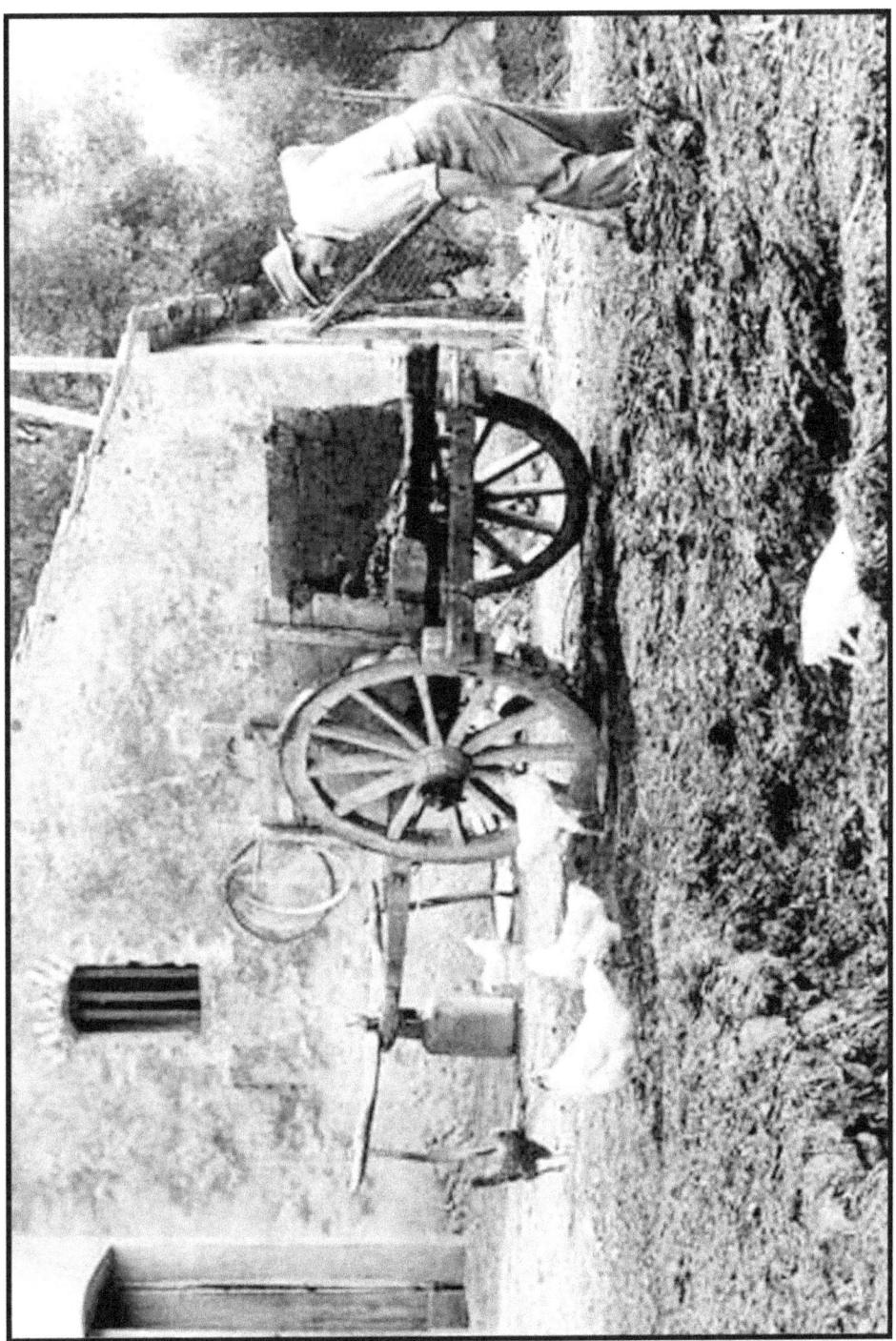

1981 – S. Onofrio (VV) – Farmer with cart – Minolta XD - FP4 – Devel. Rodinal

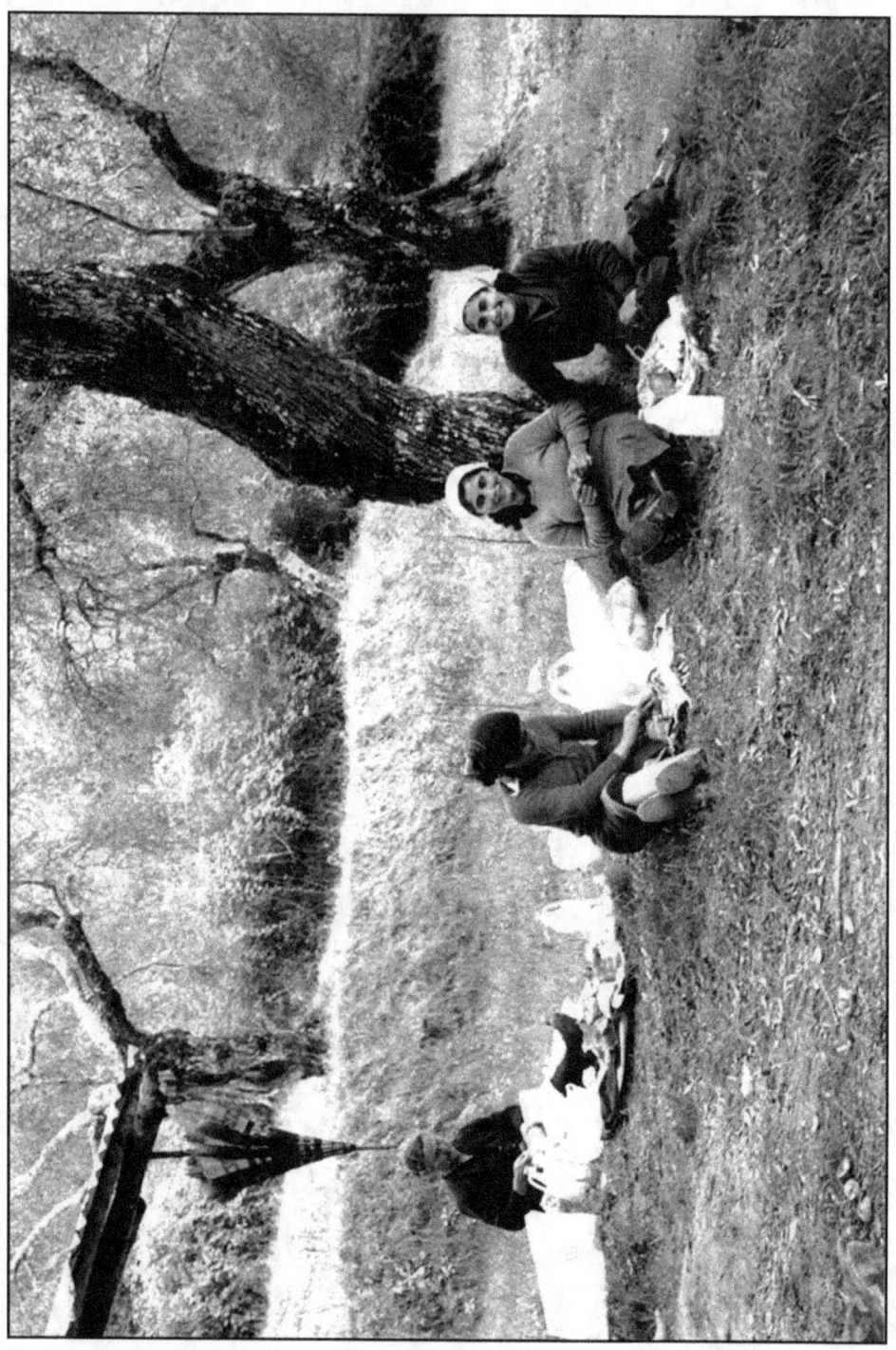

1981 - Soriano (VV) – Olive pickers - Minolta XD - FP4 – Devel. Rodinal

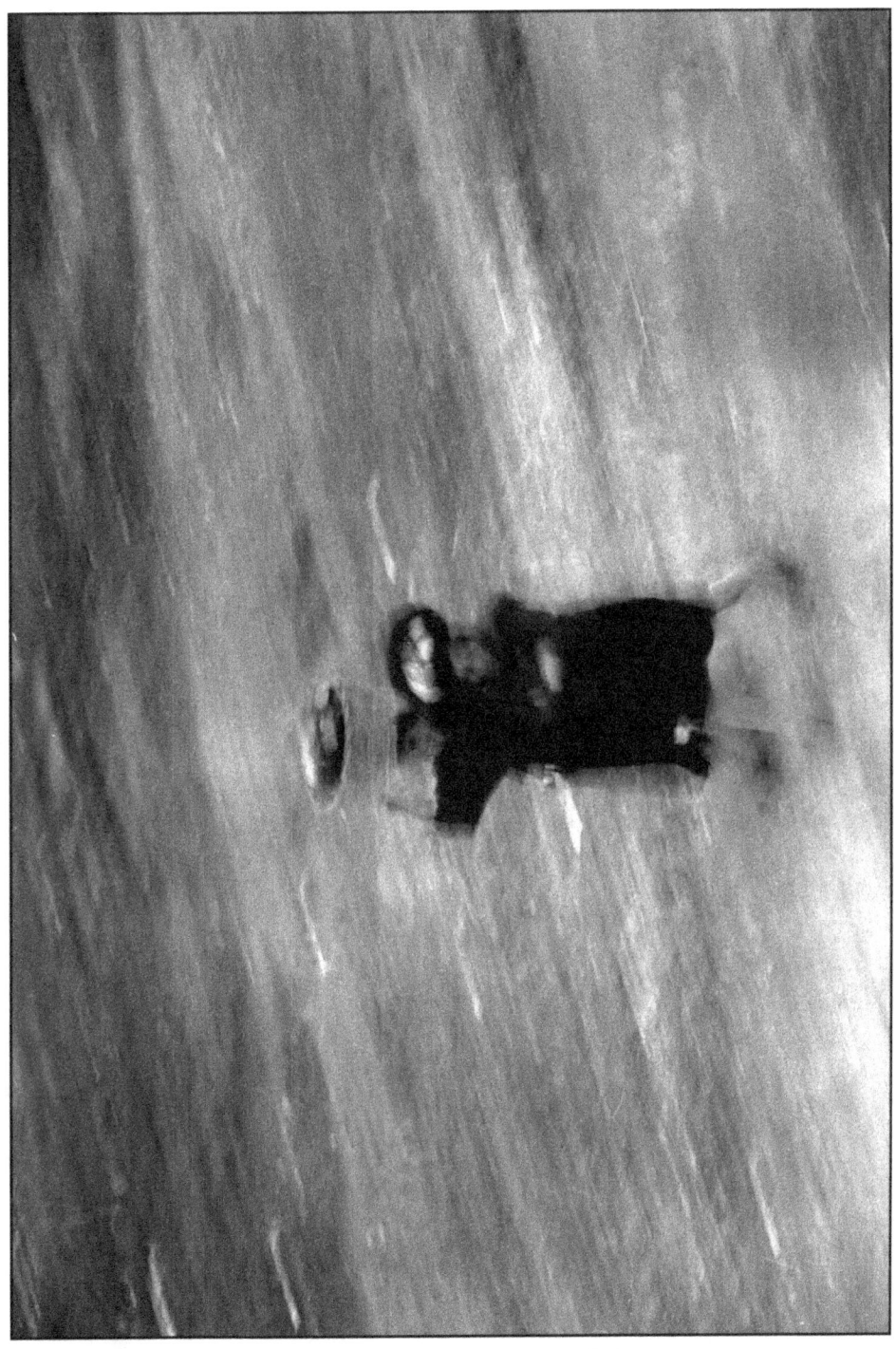

1977 - Filadelfia (VV) – Women with baskets - Minolta XD - FP4 - Devel. D76

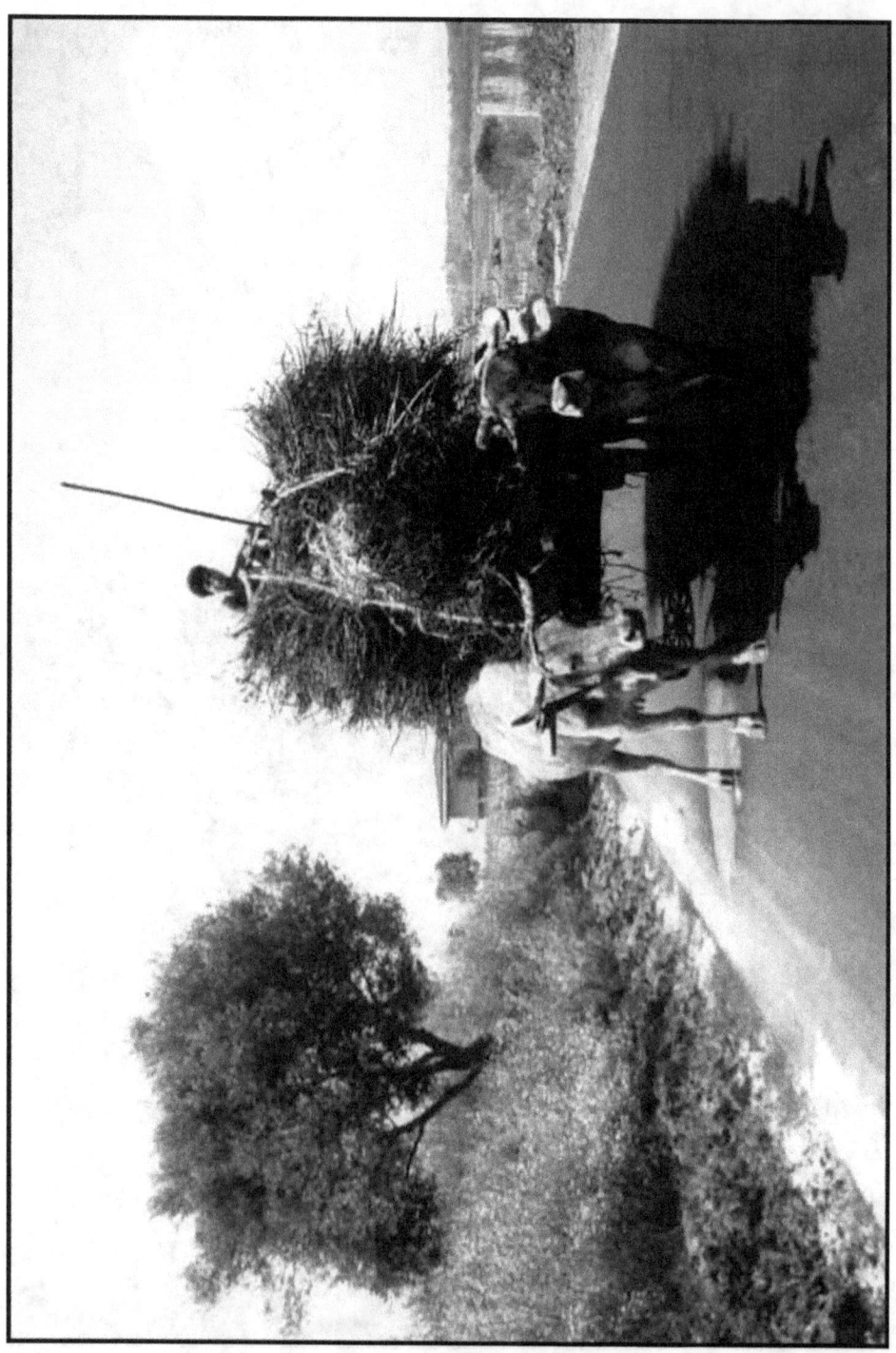

1977 – Vibo Valentia – Farmer with cart - Minolta XD - FP4 - Devel. D76

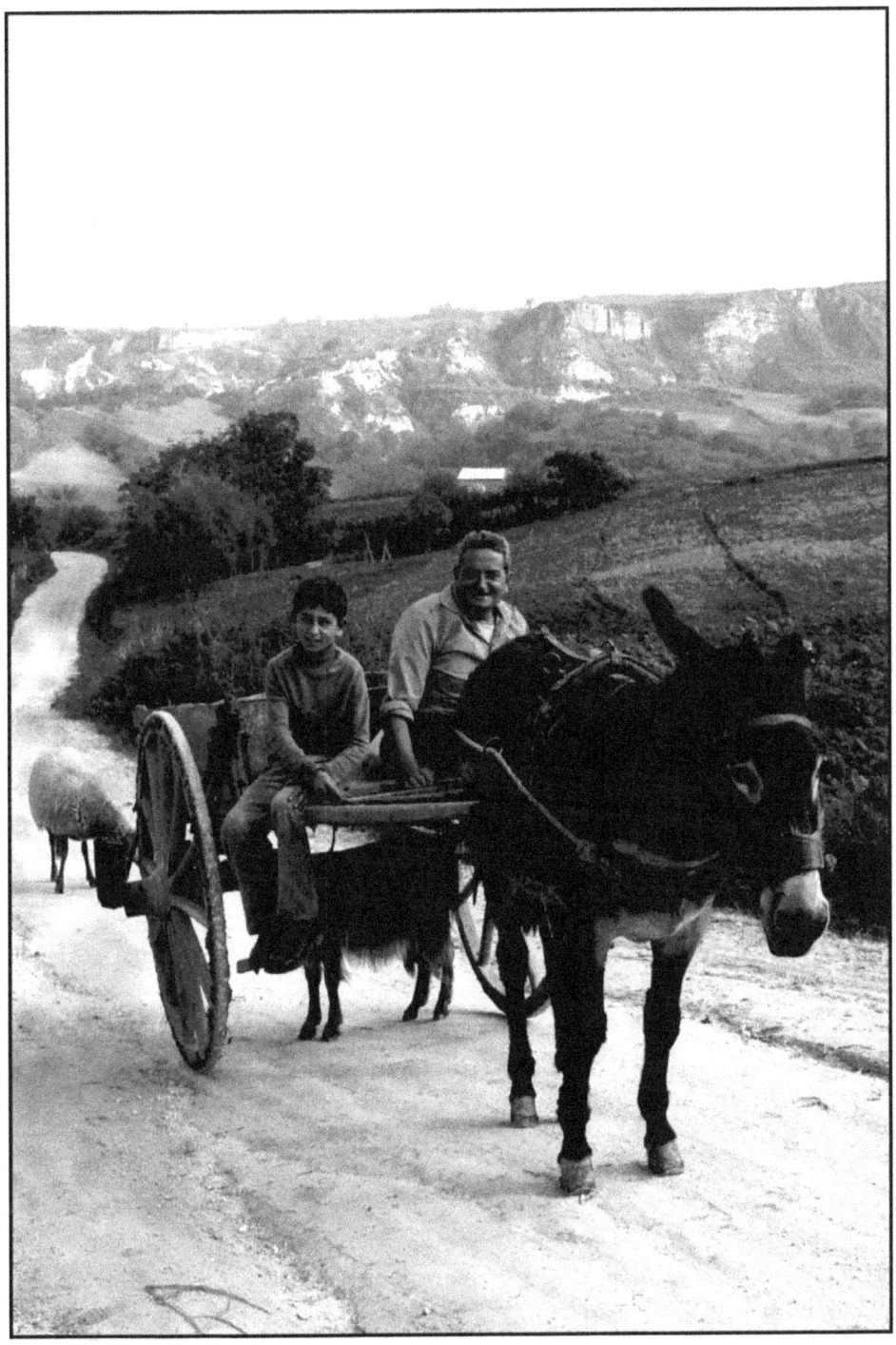

1978 - Homecoming - Koroll 35 - Ferrania P3 - Devel. Rodinal

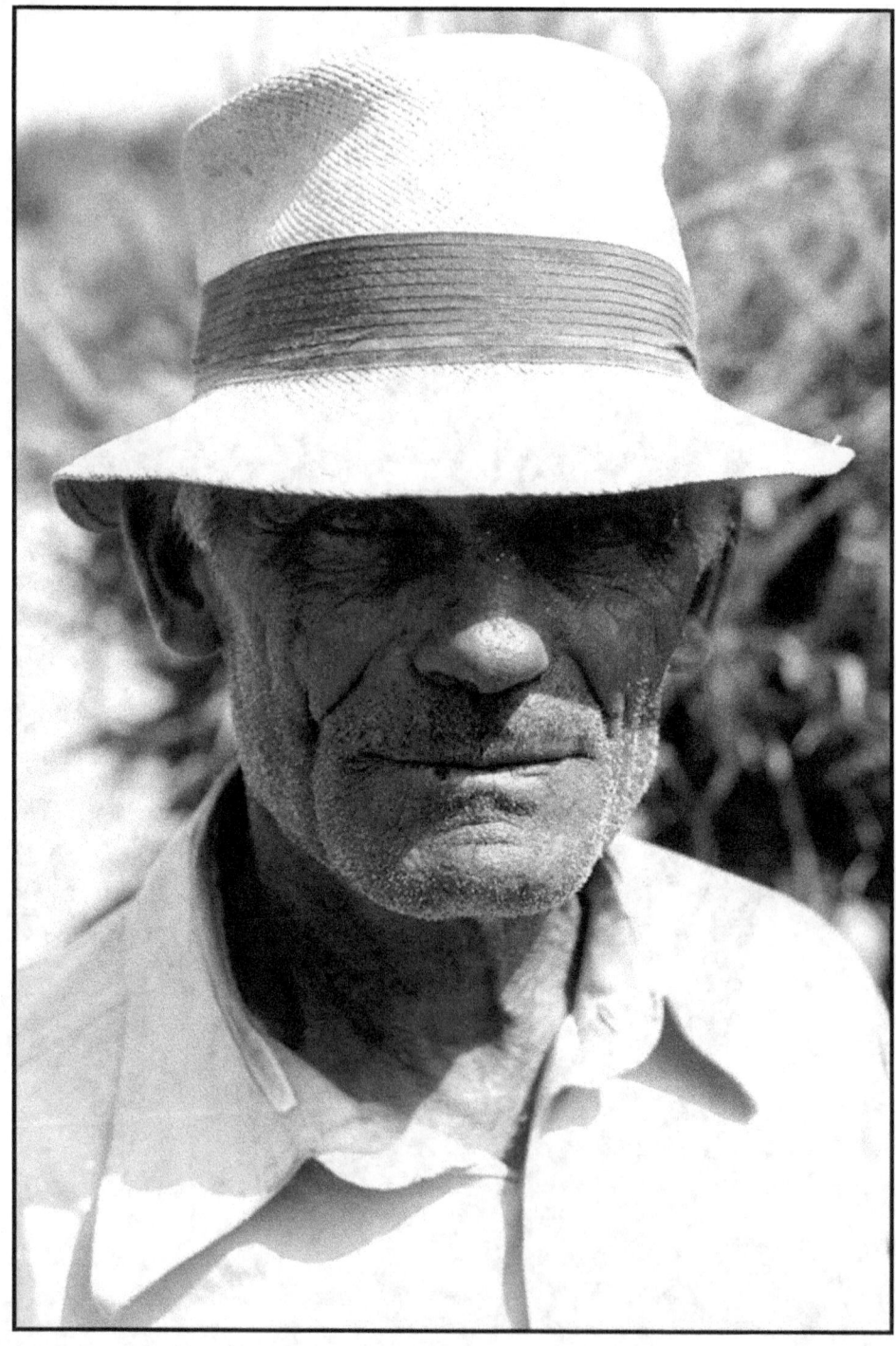

1978 - S. Angelo (VV) – Calabrian farmer - Koroll 35 - Ferrania P3 – Devel. Rodinal

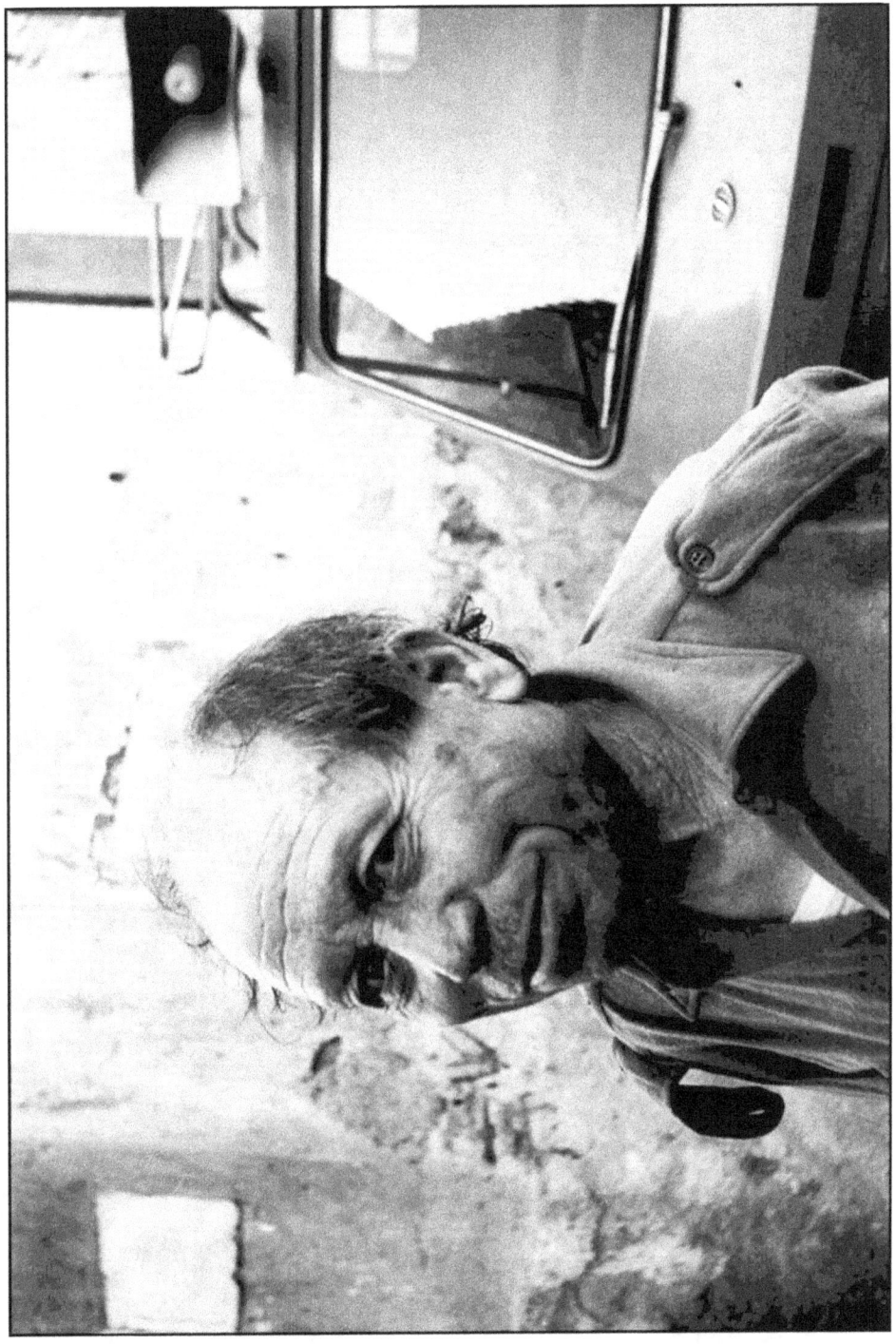

1977 - Limpidi (VV) – Calabrian farmer - Minolta XD - FP4 - Devel. D76

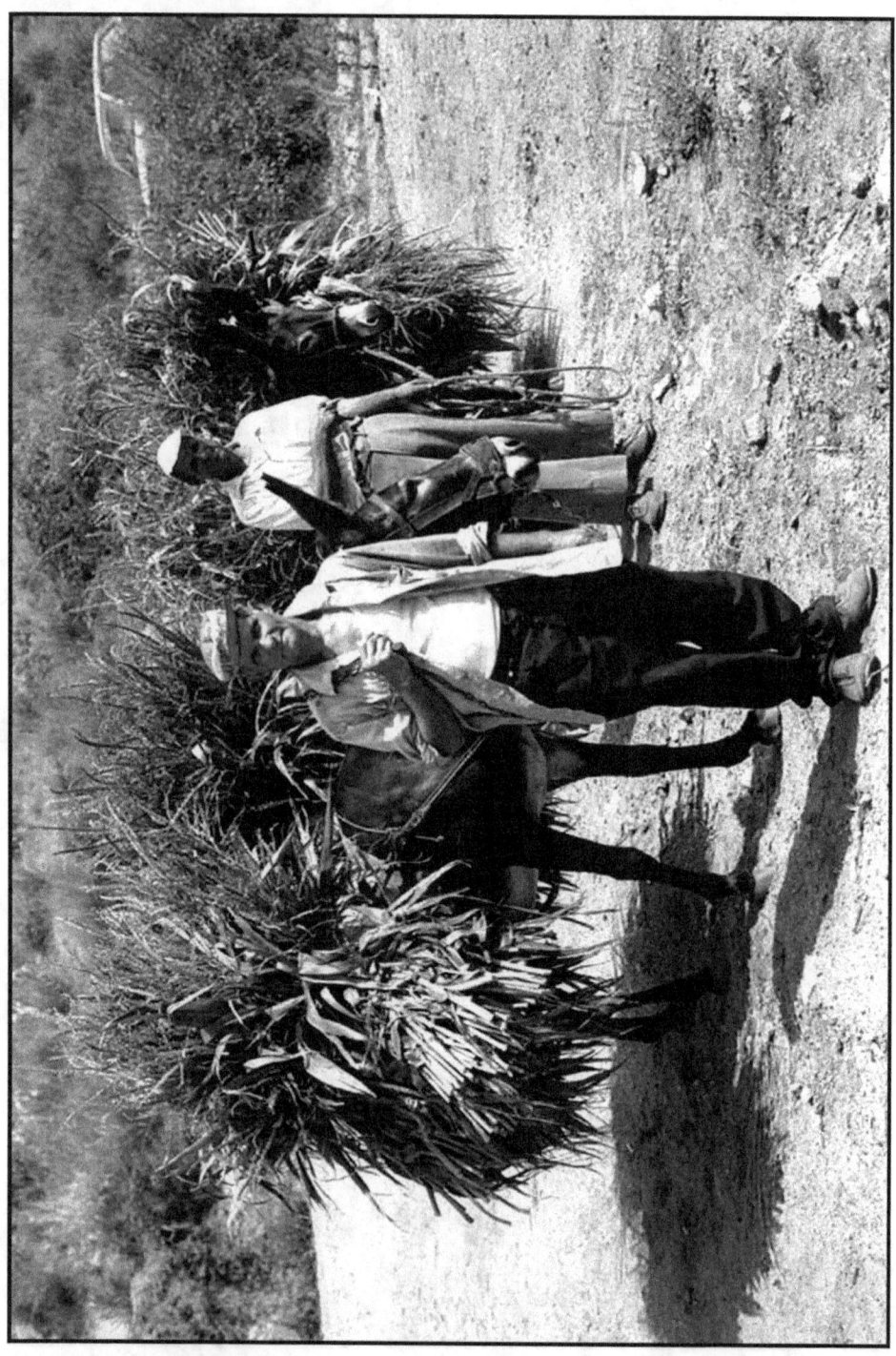

1978 – The donkeys - Koroll 35 - Ferrania P3 - Devel. Agfa Rodinal

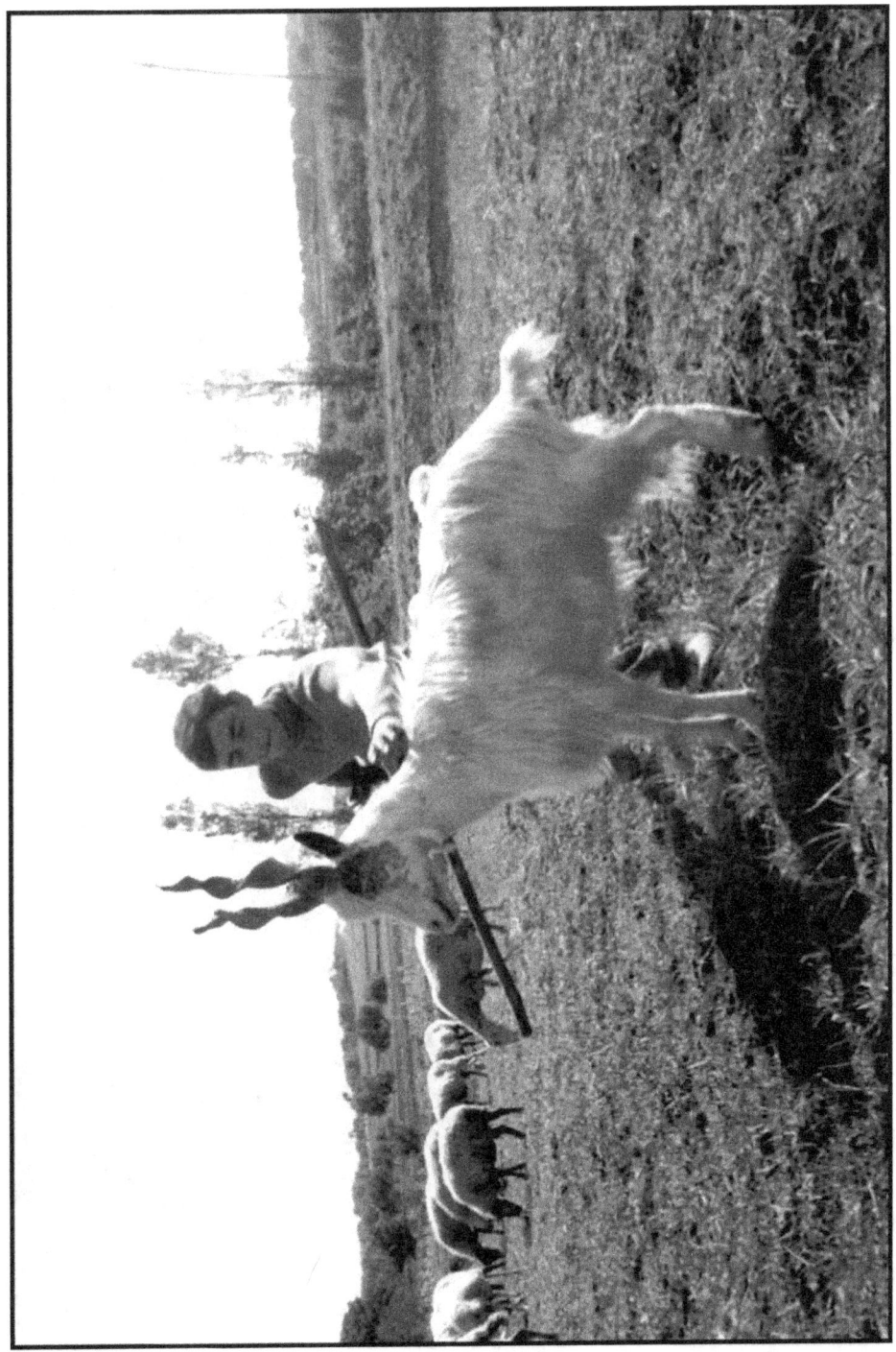

1978 – Serra S. Bruno (VV) – Calabrian shepherd - MinoltaXD - FP4 - Devel. D76

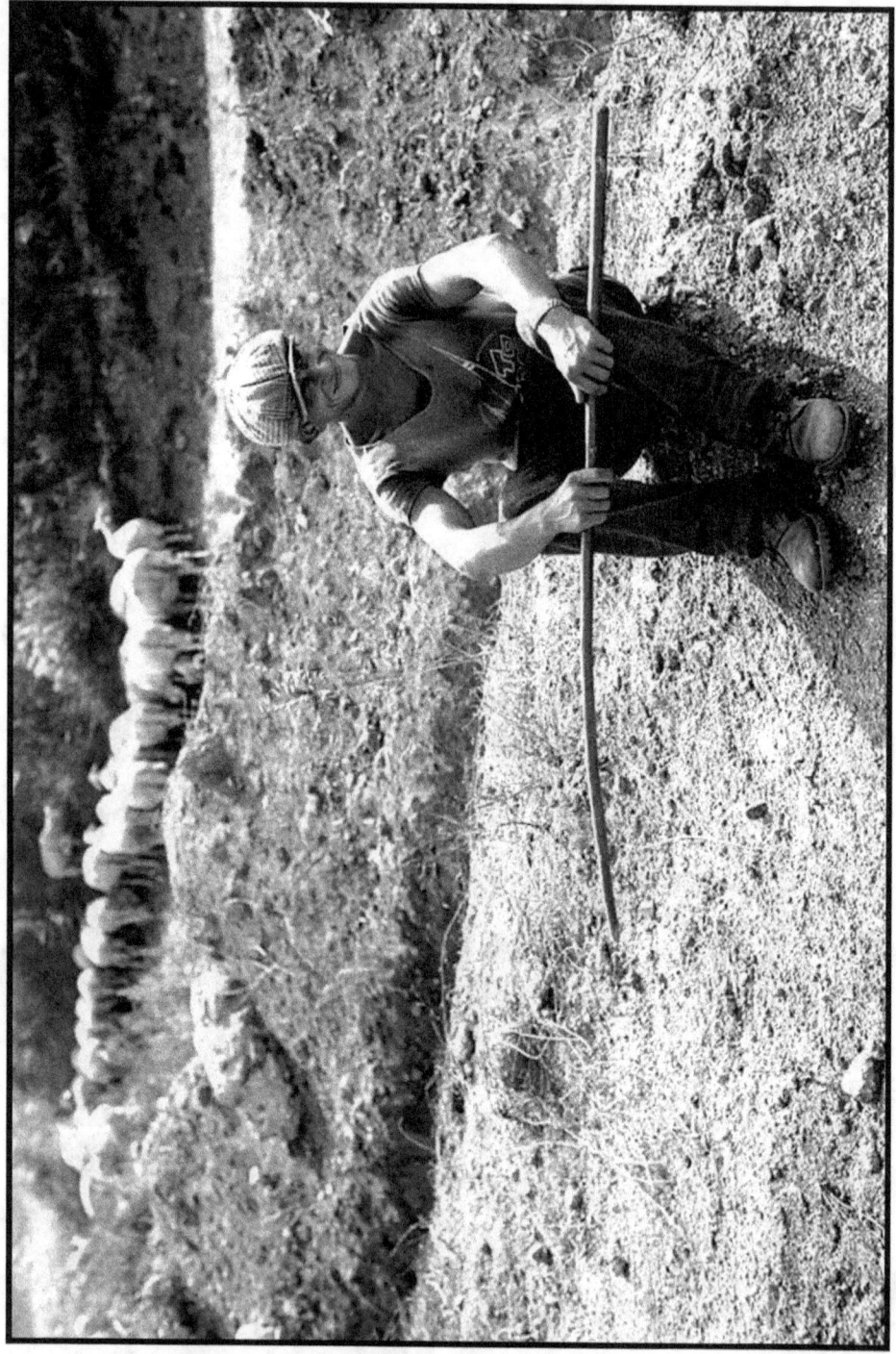

1978 – Serra S. Bruno (VV) - Calabrian shepherd - MinoltaXD - FP4 - Devel. D76

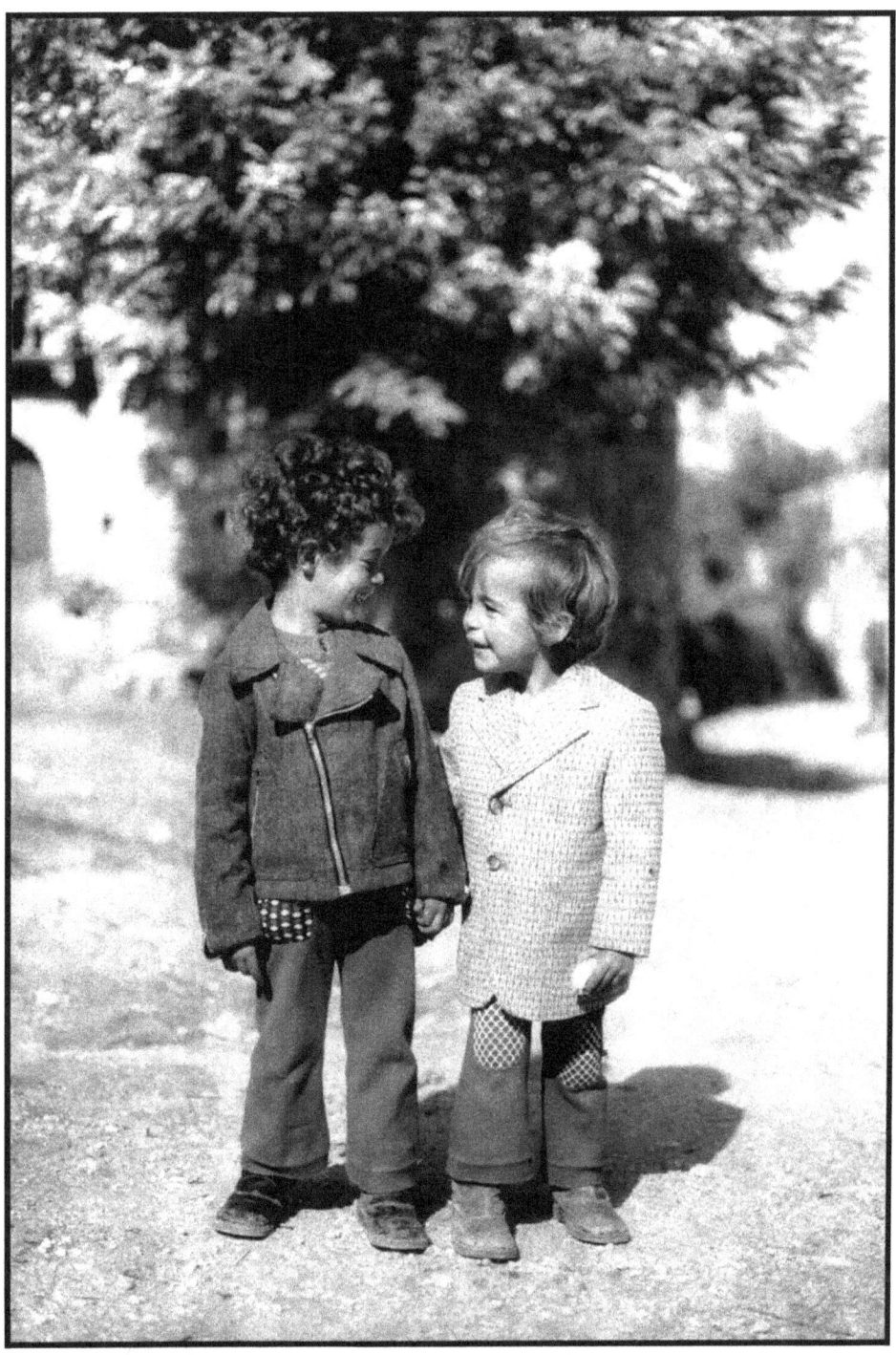

1977 – Papaglionti (VV) - Children - Minolta XD - FP4 – Devel. D76

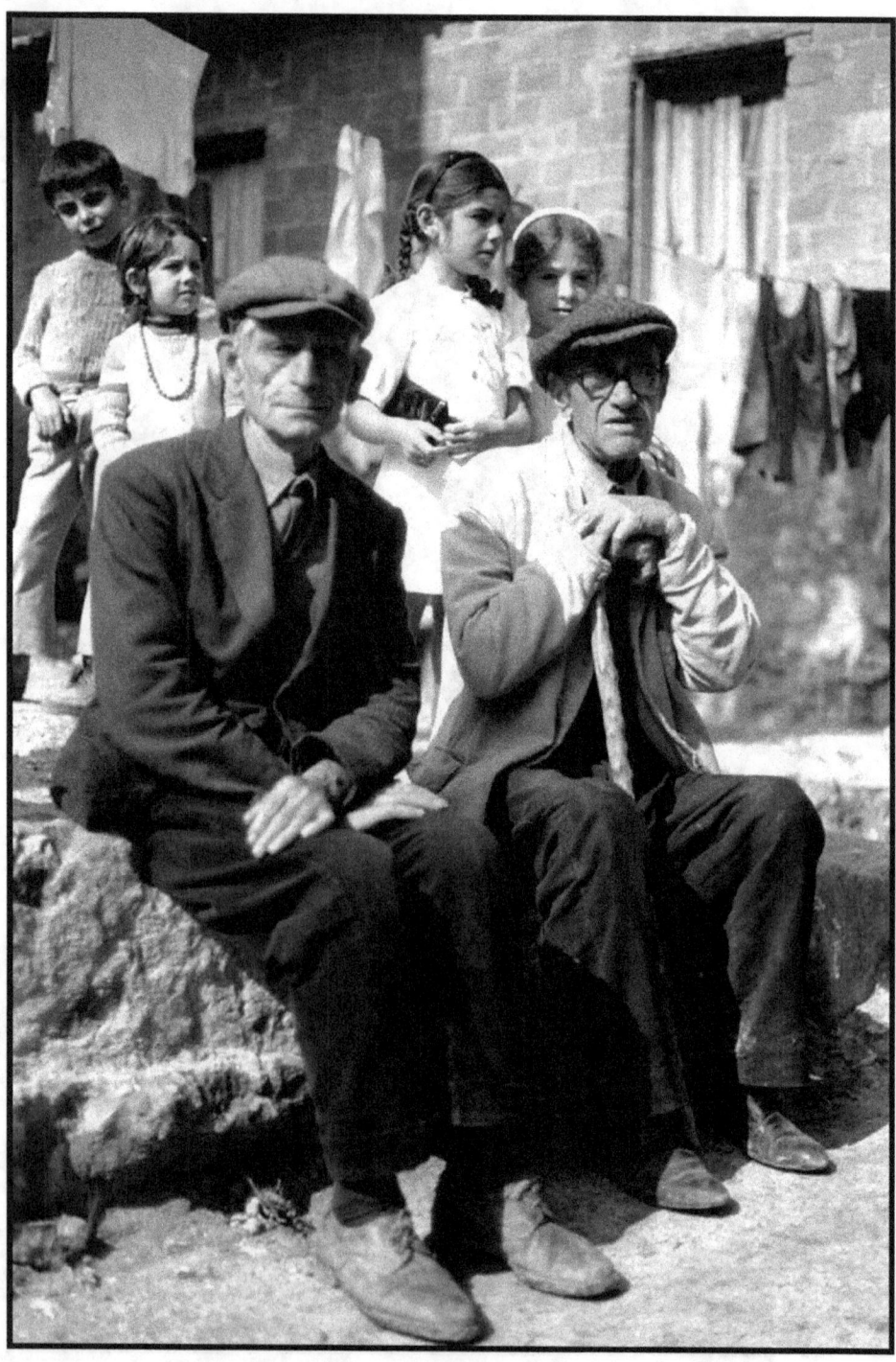

1977 – Papaglionti (VV) - Elderly in the sun - Minolta XD - FP4 - Devel. D76

FOTOART

*

FOTOART

*

4 SYMBOLIC PHOTO

Those who have sought in the things that are part of life, the essence of the same, to grasp what goes beyond the value of appearance, comes to appreciate the strength of the symbol and penetrates an unusual truth.

The symbol is the bearer of concepts that become the vehicle of discovery of the recondite reality that sediments in the consciousness of every man.

The symbol has no doctrine, no dogma, no philosophical system; is only an "initium" of the process that the interiority, in its basic freedom, must implement so the pure reality received and discovered, is above the relative truths and all temporary things.

FOTOART

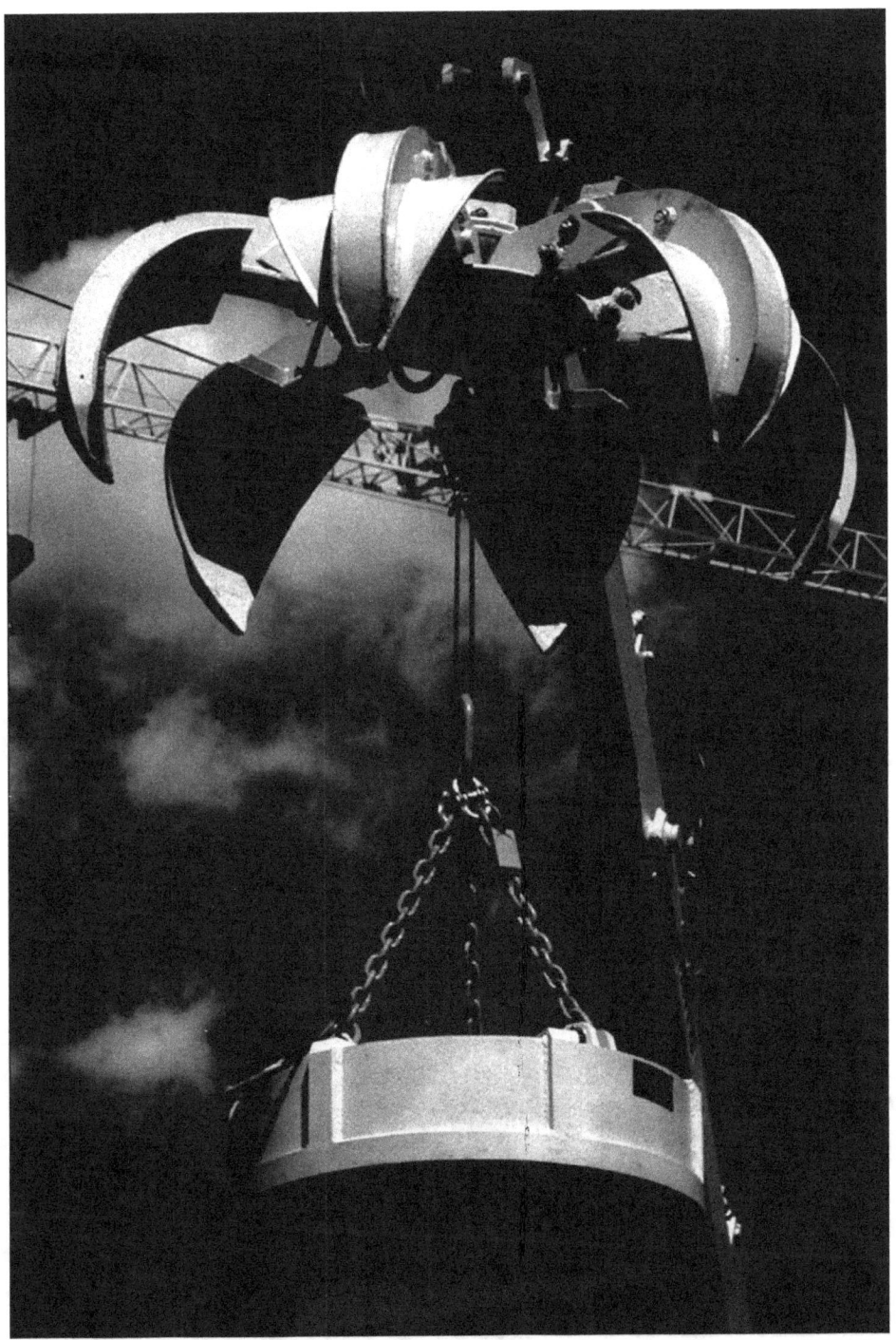

1976 – Milan Fair (MI) - Magnetic crane – Olympus OM1 - Ilford FP4 - Devel. Ilfosol

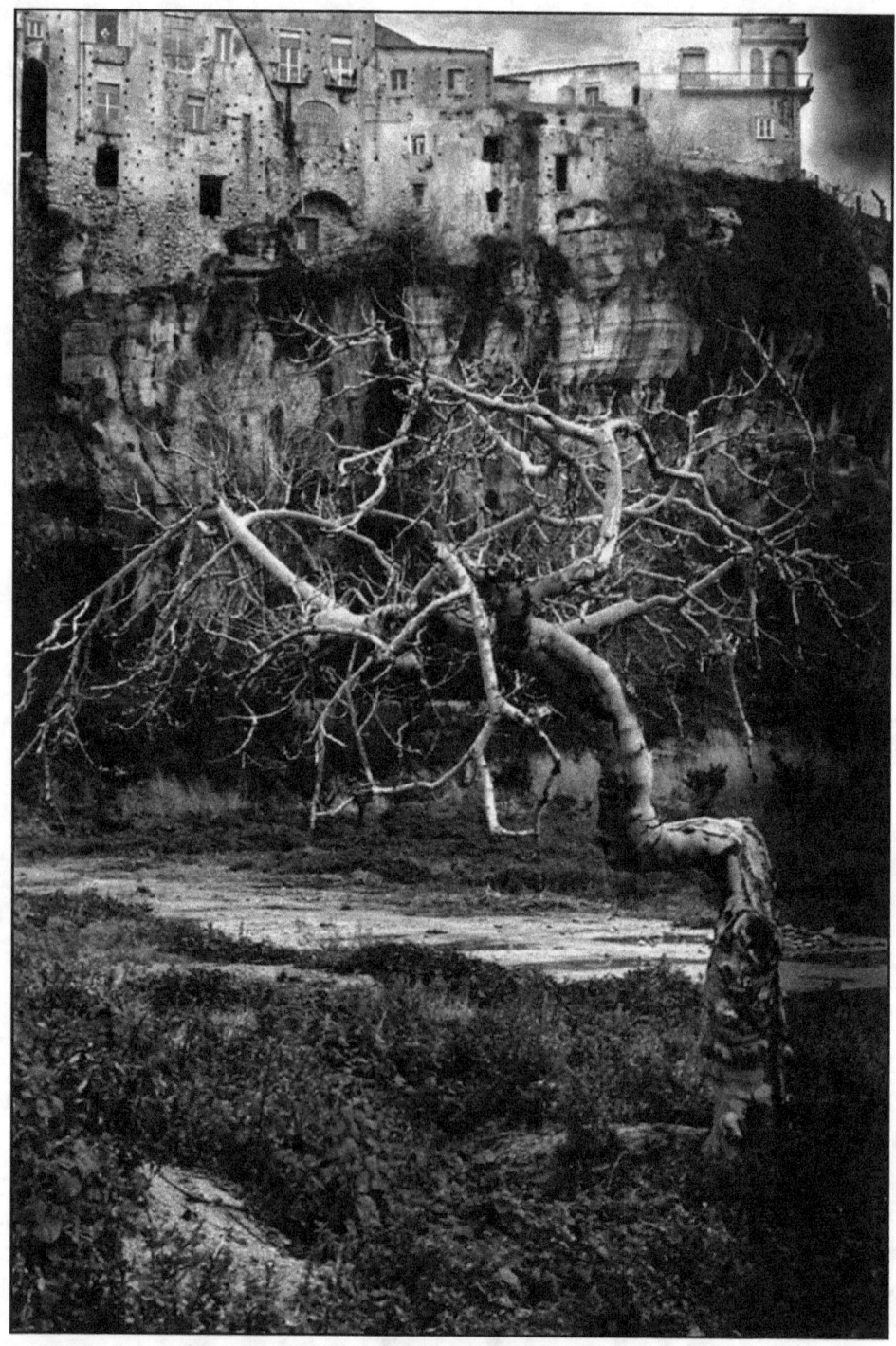

1981 - Tropea (VV) - Olympus OM1 - Ilford FP4 - Devel. ID11

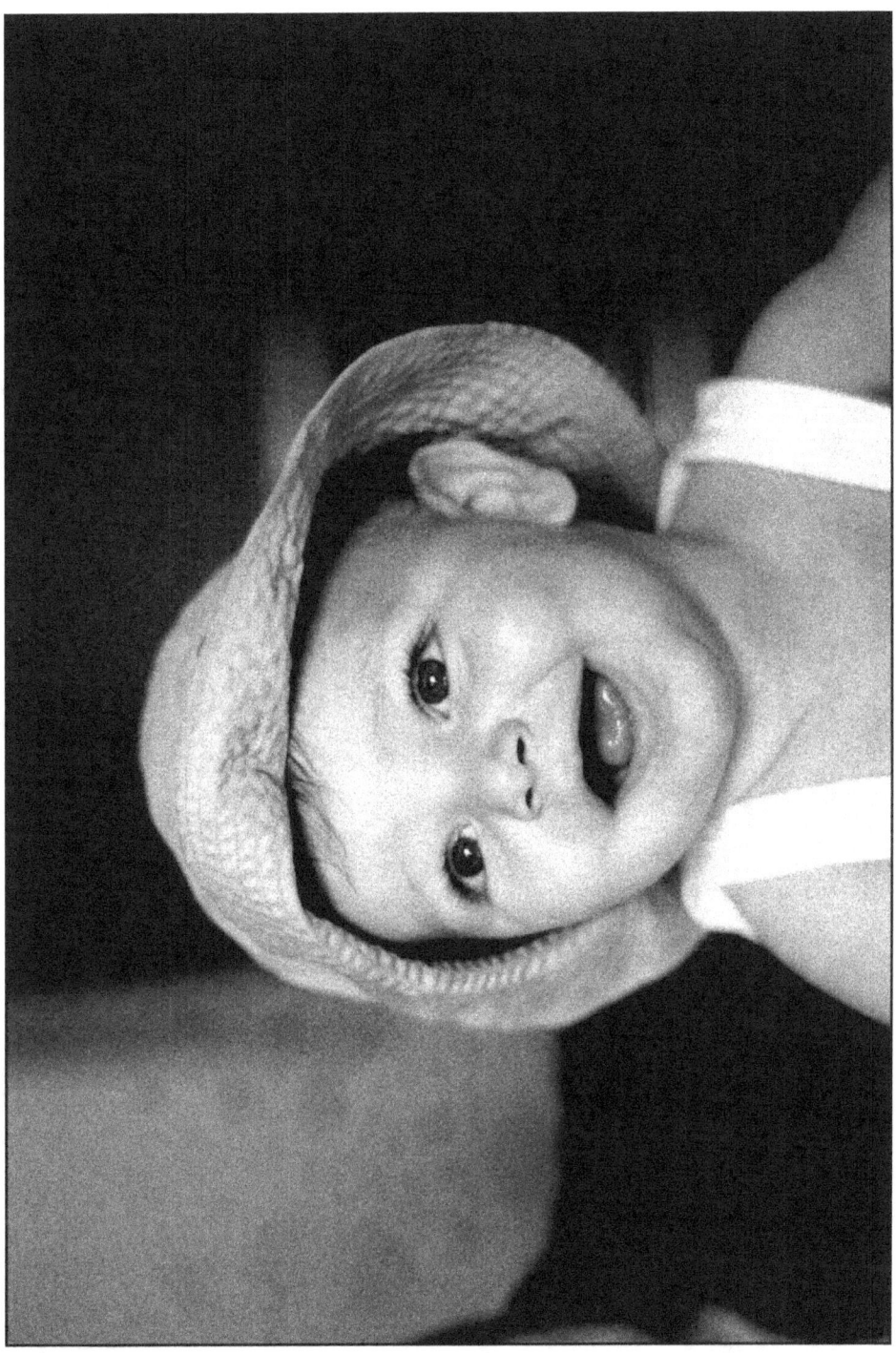

1979 - Milan - Portrait - Olympus OM1 - Ilford HP5 - Devel. Microphen

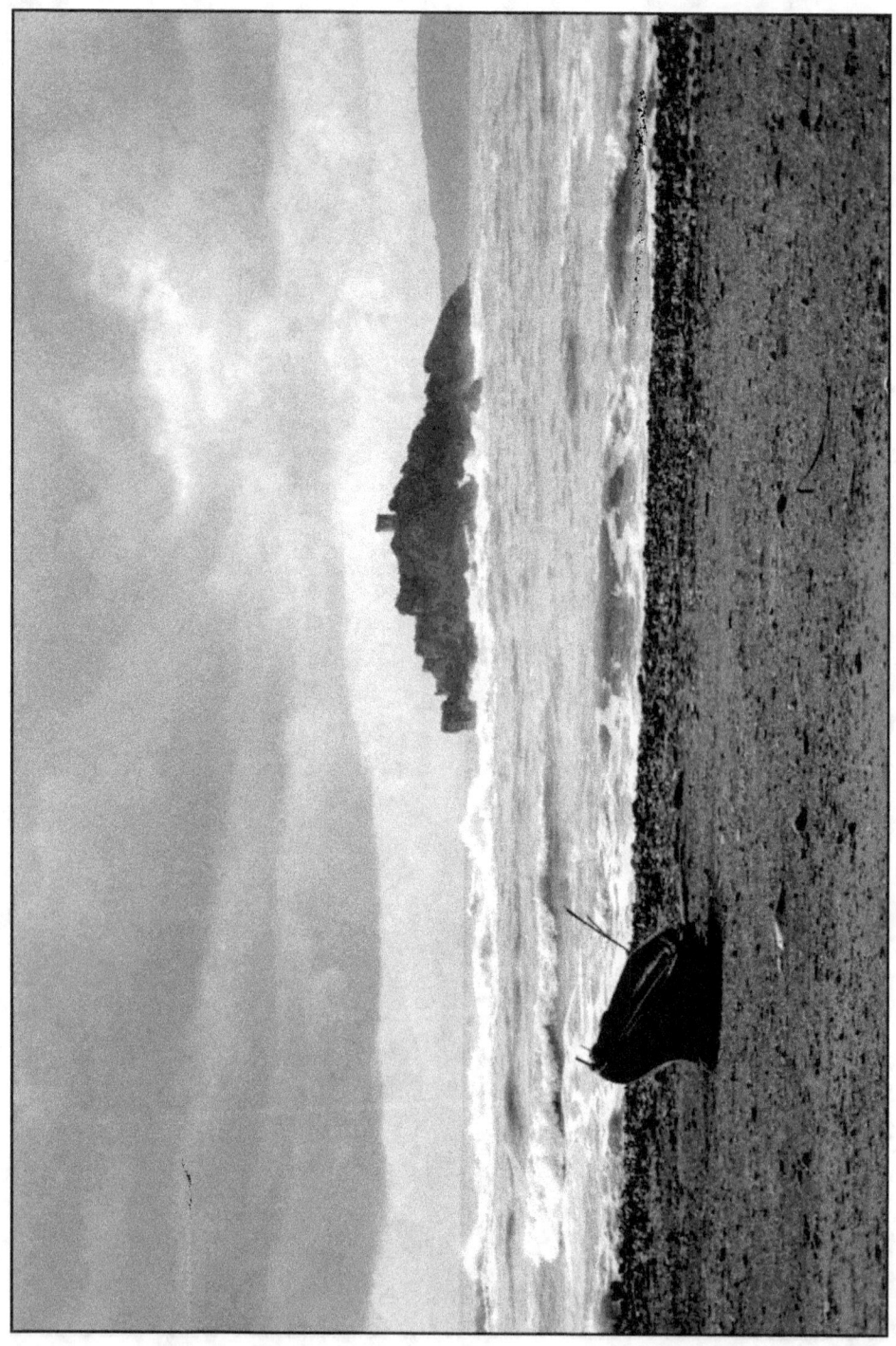

1977 – Punta Ala (GR) - Island – Minolta XD - FP4 - Devel. D76

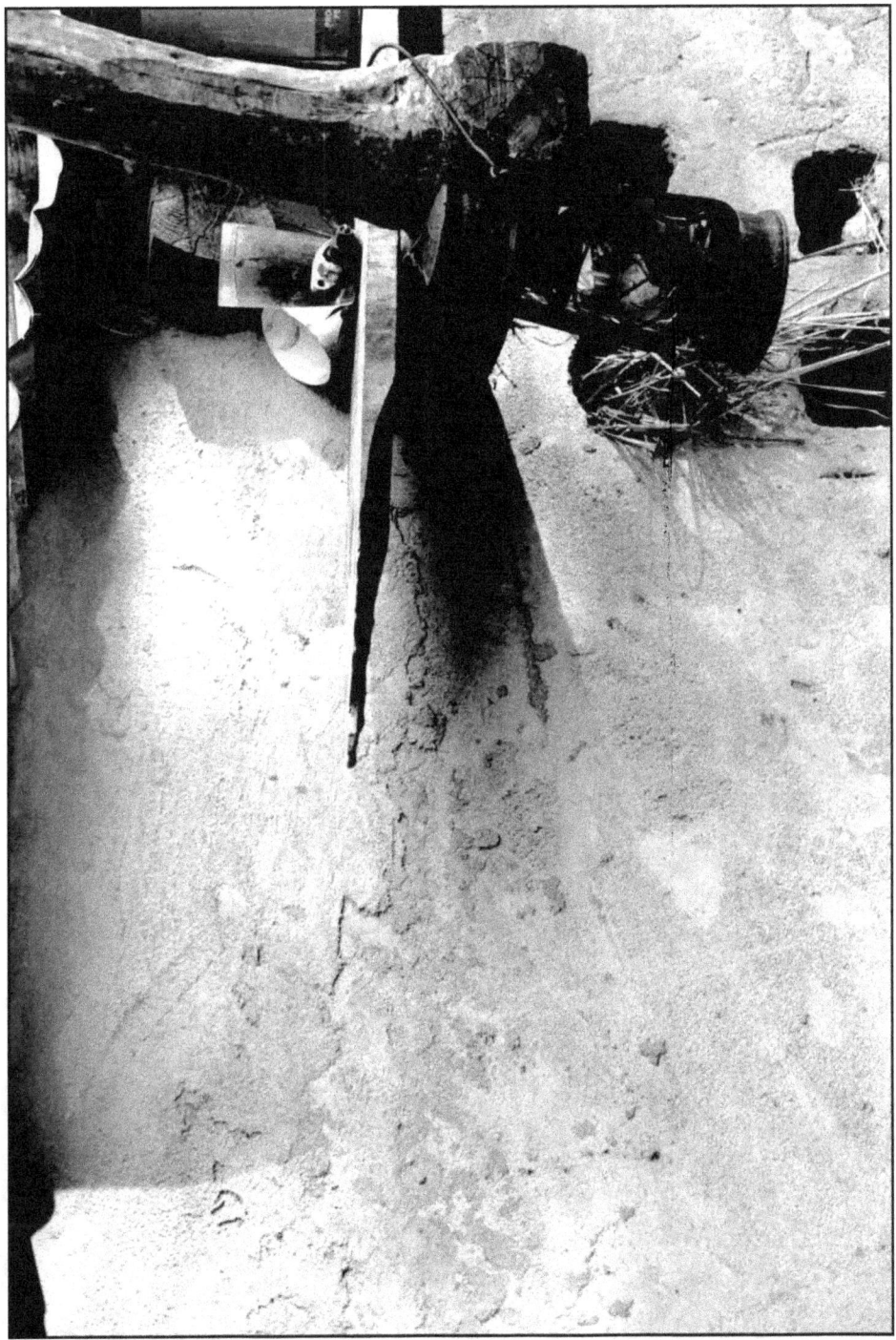

1970 - S. Onofrio (VV) – The lantern - Ferrania P3 – Manual development similar to ID11

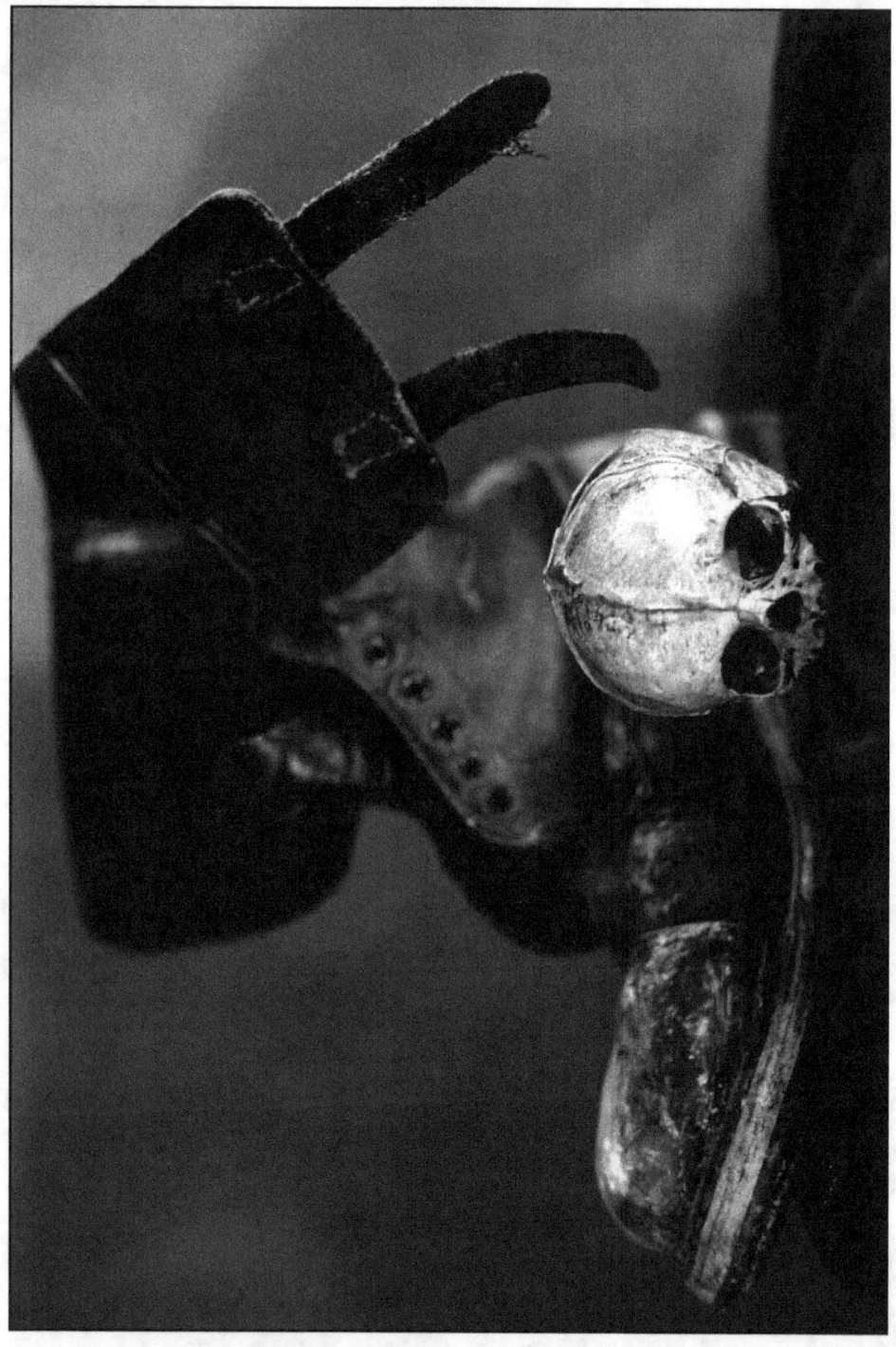

1973 – The wars ugliness - Ferrania P3 - Manual development similar to ID11

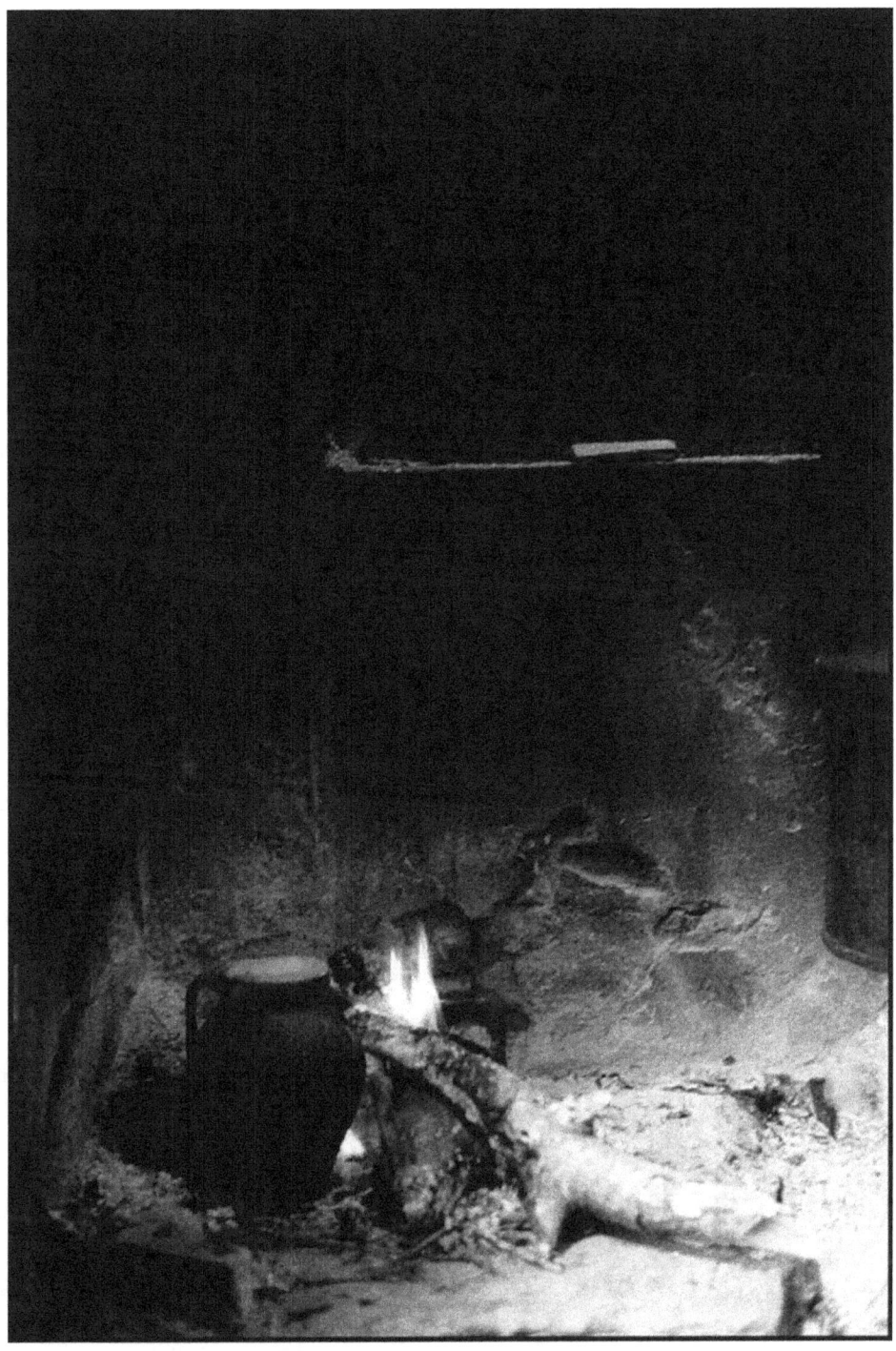

1979 – Limpidi (VV)- The beans - Koroll 35 - Ferrania P3 – Devel. Rodinal

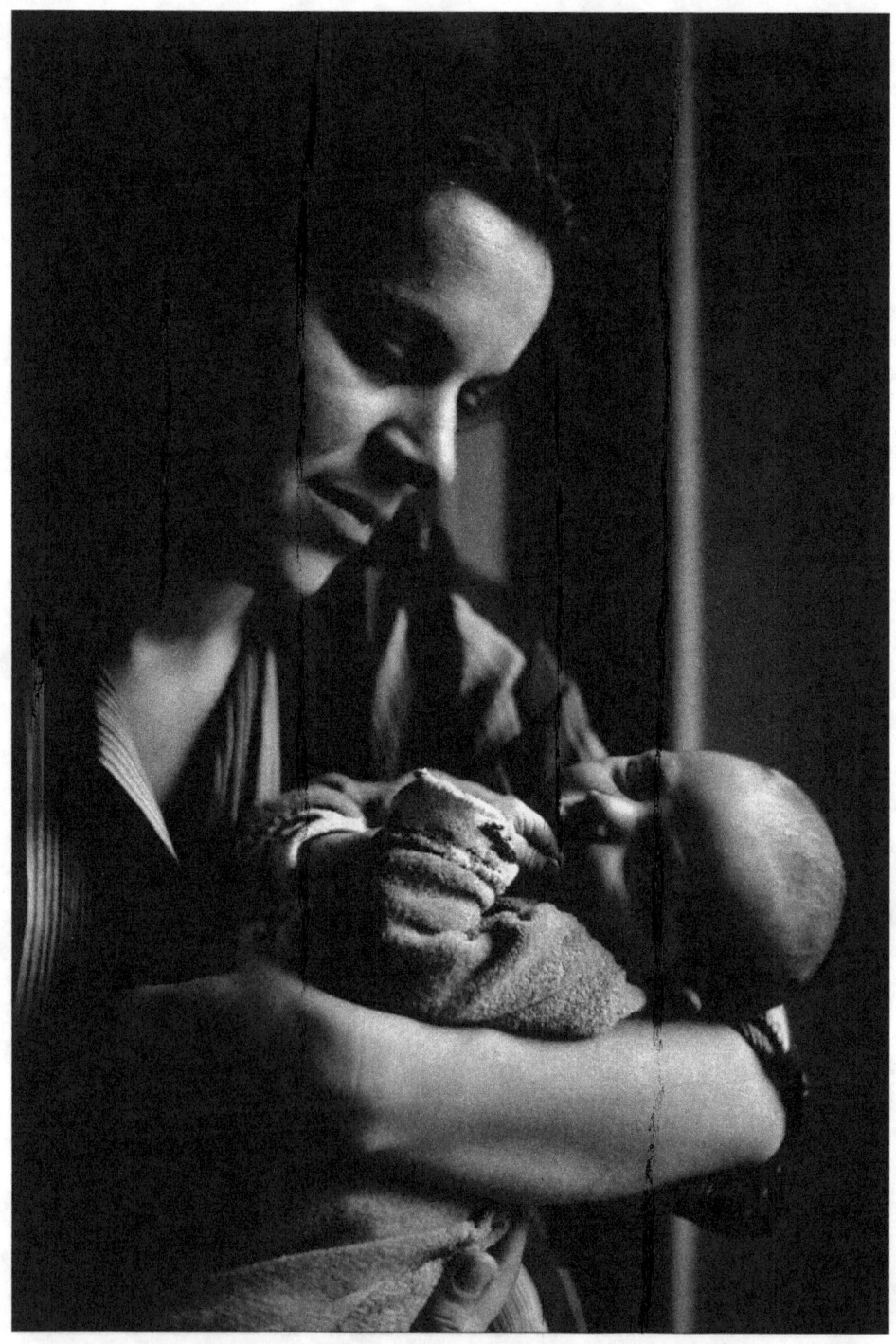

1978 – Maternity - Olympus OM1 - Ilford FP4 - Devel. Microphen

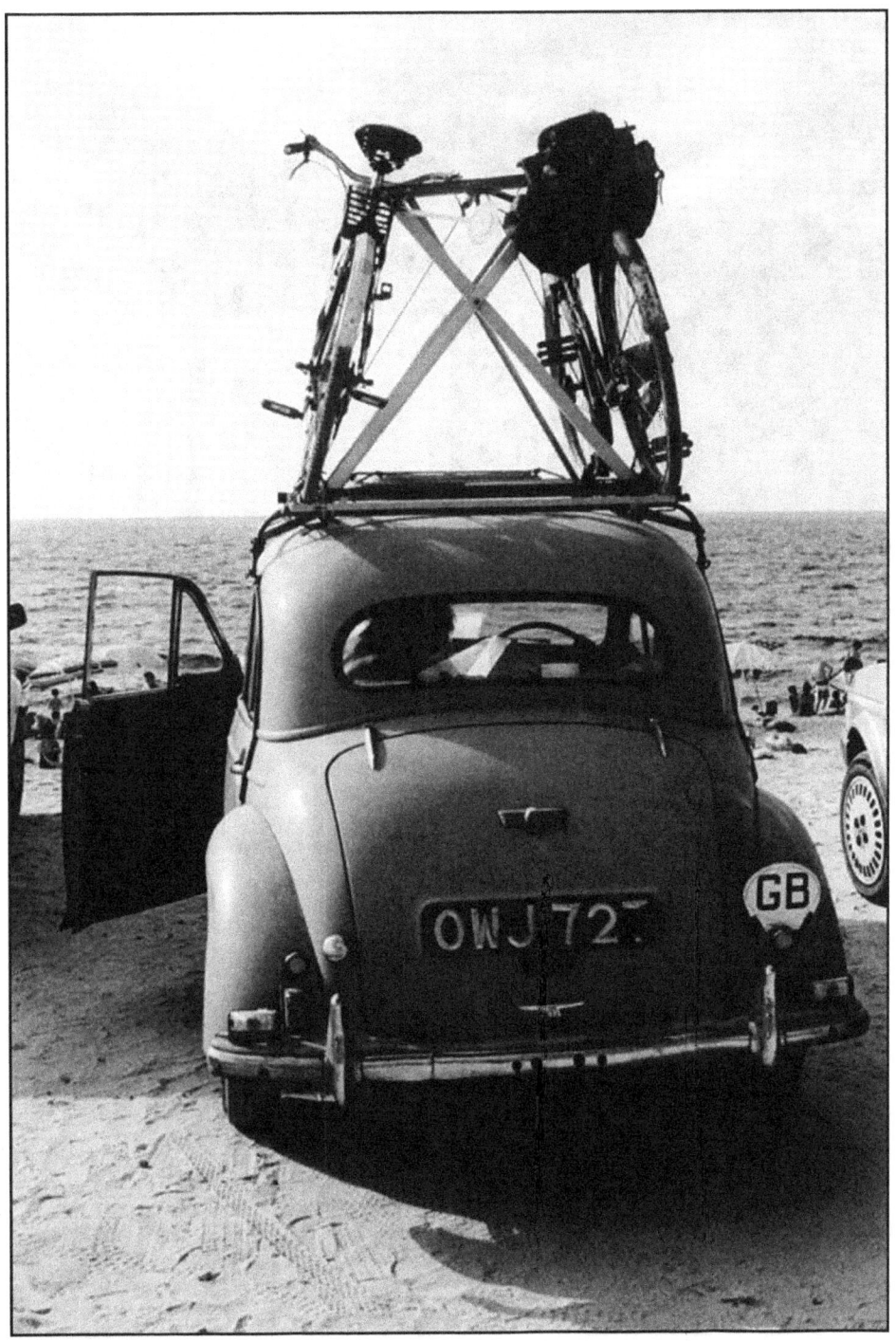

1980 – Briatico (VV) - English car - Minolta XD - FP4 - Devel. D76

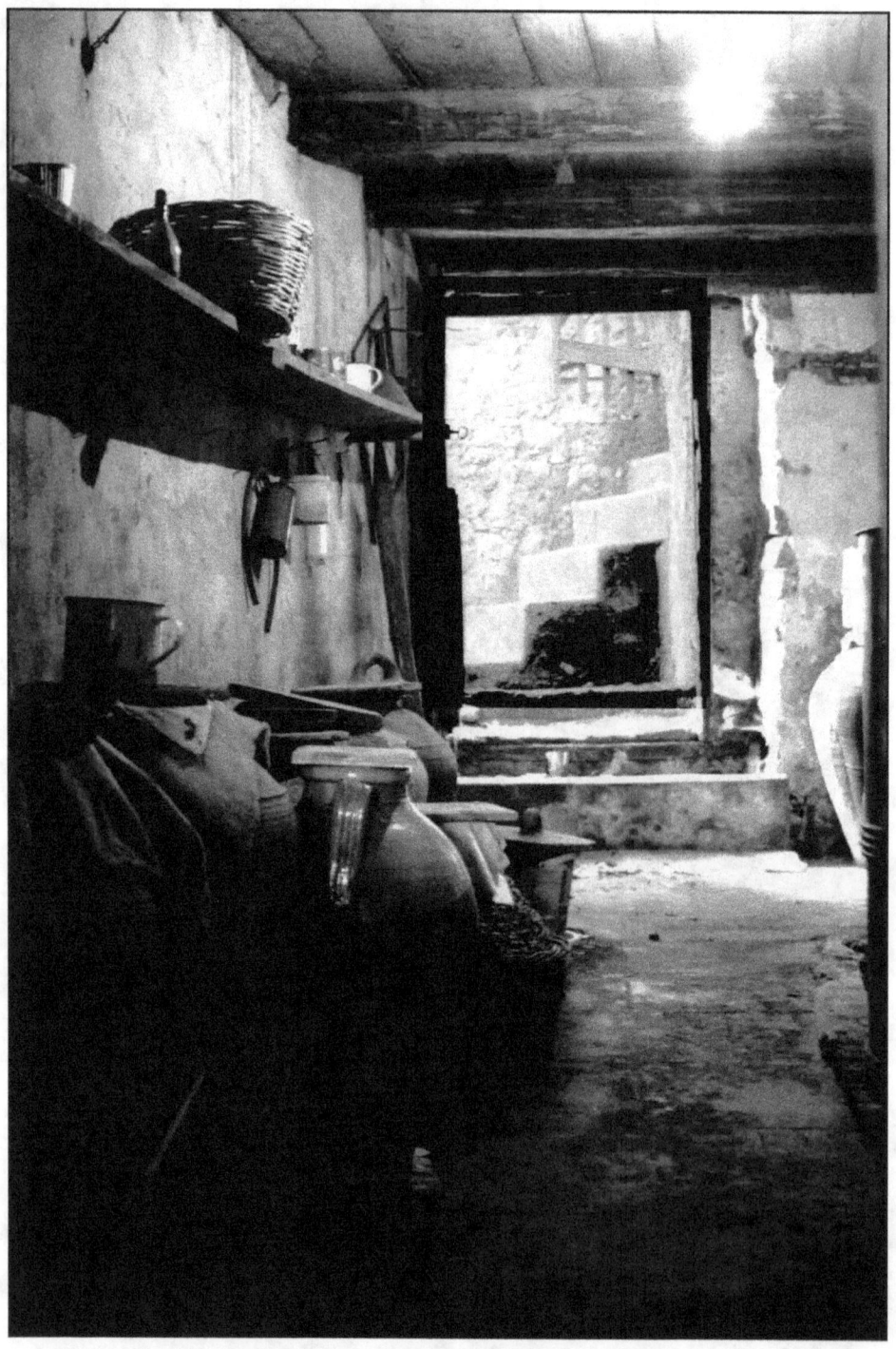

1972 – Cellar - Olympus OM1 - Ilford FP4 - Devel. Microphen

FOTOART

*

5 THE EXTRAORDINARY NATURE OF SIMPLE THINGS

Driven by the speed of modern life, we sail in a sea of information and act in a ferment of commitments with the conscious certainty that everything flows and everything evolves relentlessly. But, when we find ourselves alone with our spirit we realize that we have nothing in hand that can enrich our inherent nature. Yet, all this, can be found in the recall of the past, in the memories aroused by the images of the time and, always, in the small and insignificant things that surround us. It is enough to feed that little spiritual spark that is in each of us to discover the great hidden and universal value of the various objective realities.

FOTOART

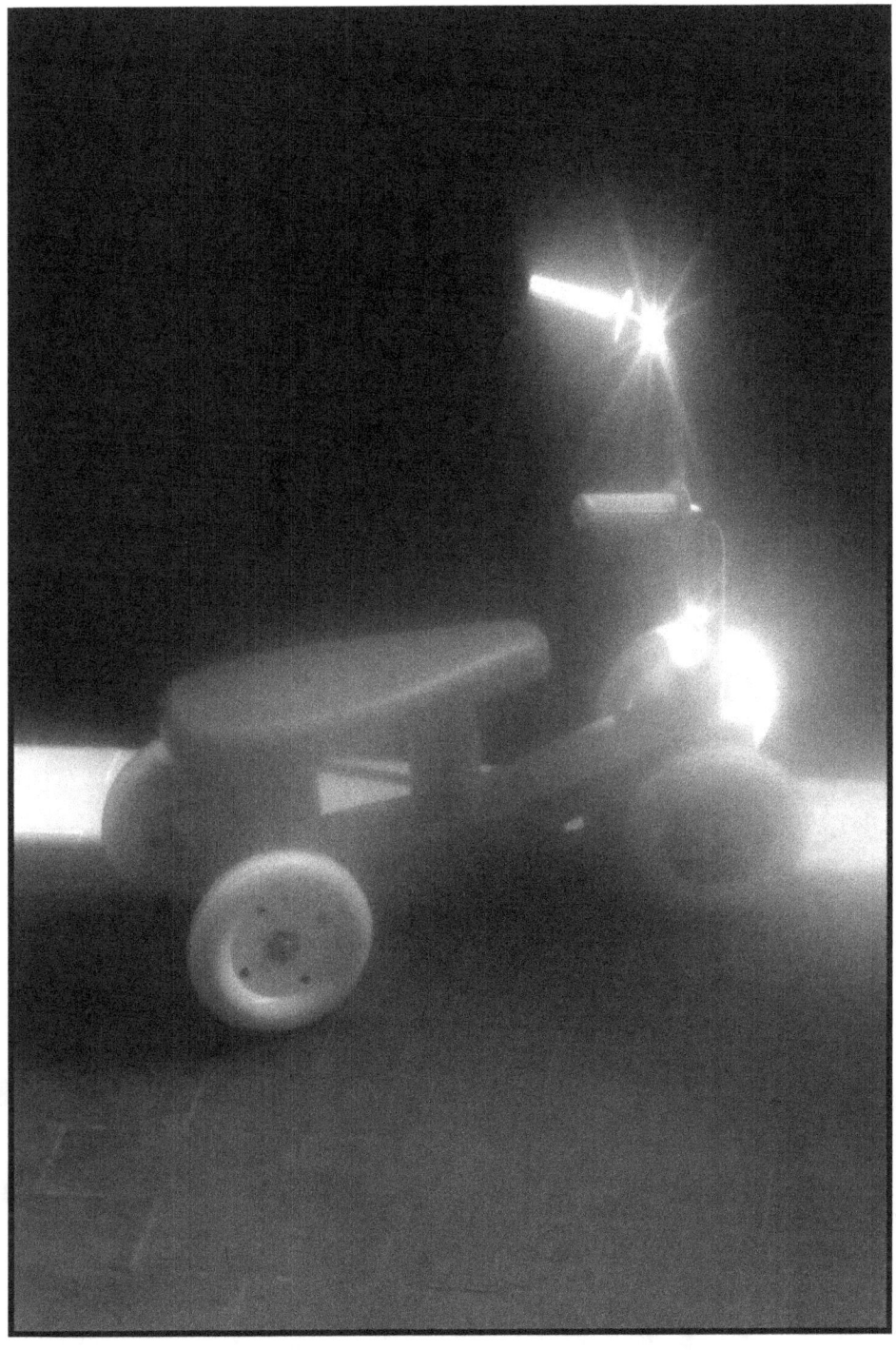

1985 – Children's bicycle - Olympus OM1 - Ilford FP4 - Devel. Microphen

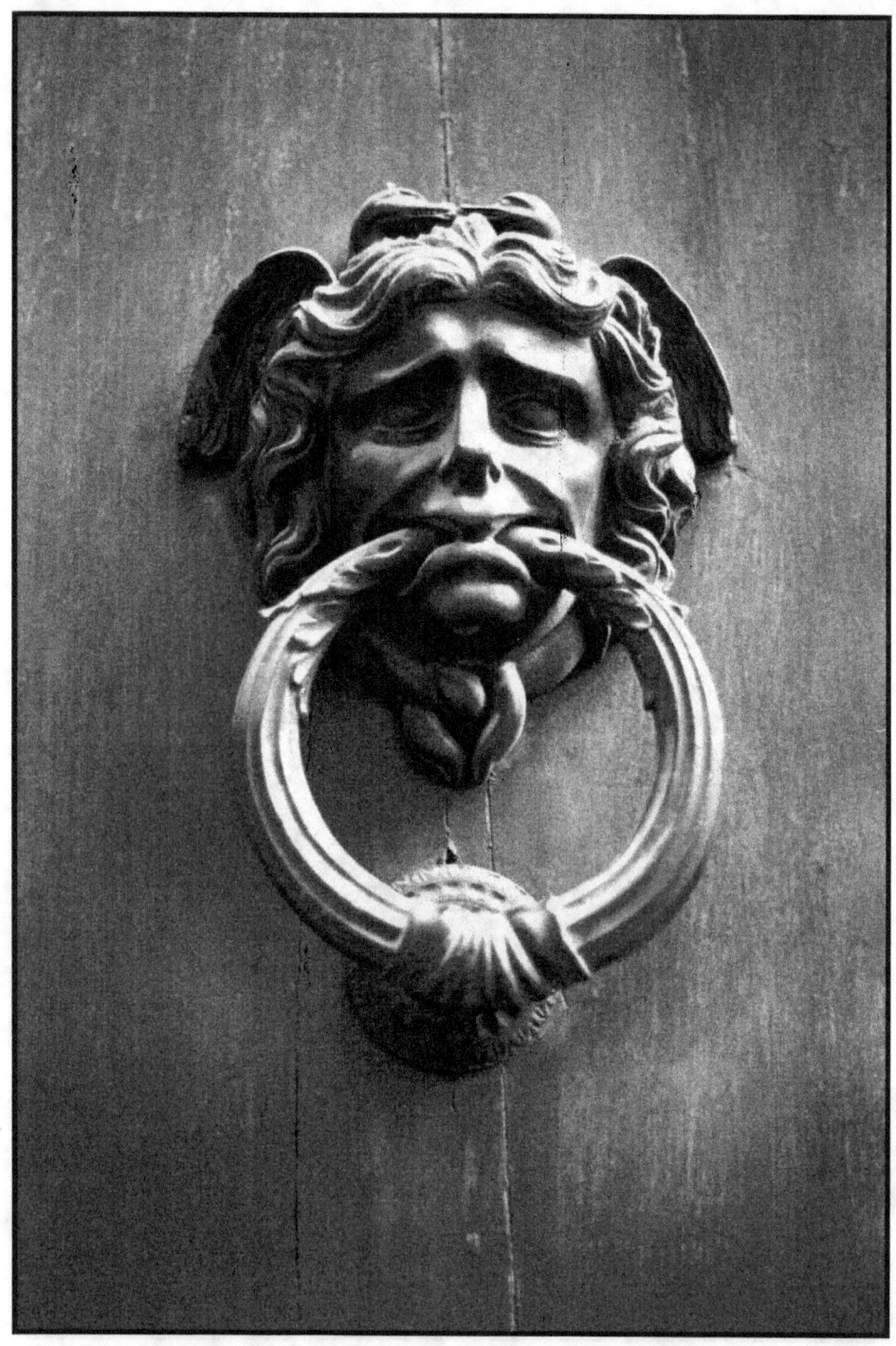

1980 – Firenze - Door knocker – Minolta XD - FP4 - Devel. D76

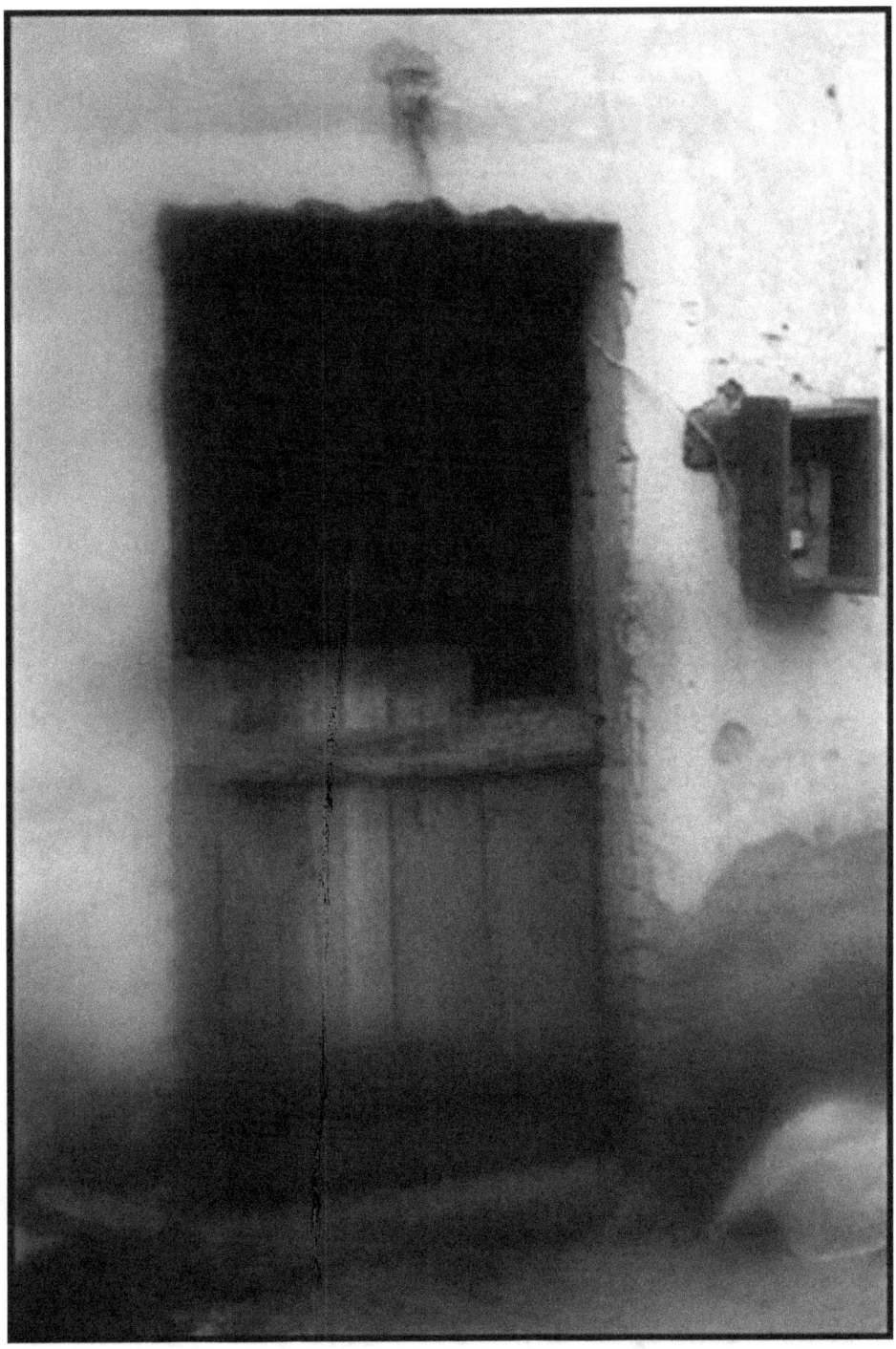

1972 – Mileto (VV) – Country gate - Olympus OM1 - Ilford FP4 - Devel. Microphen

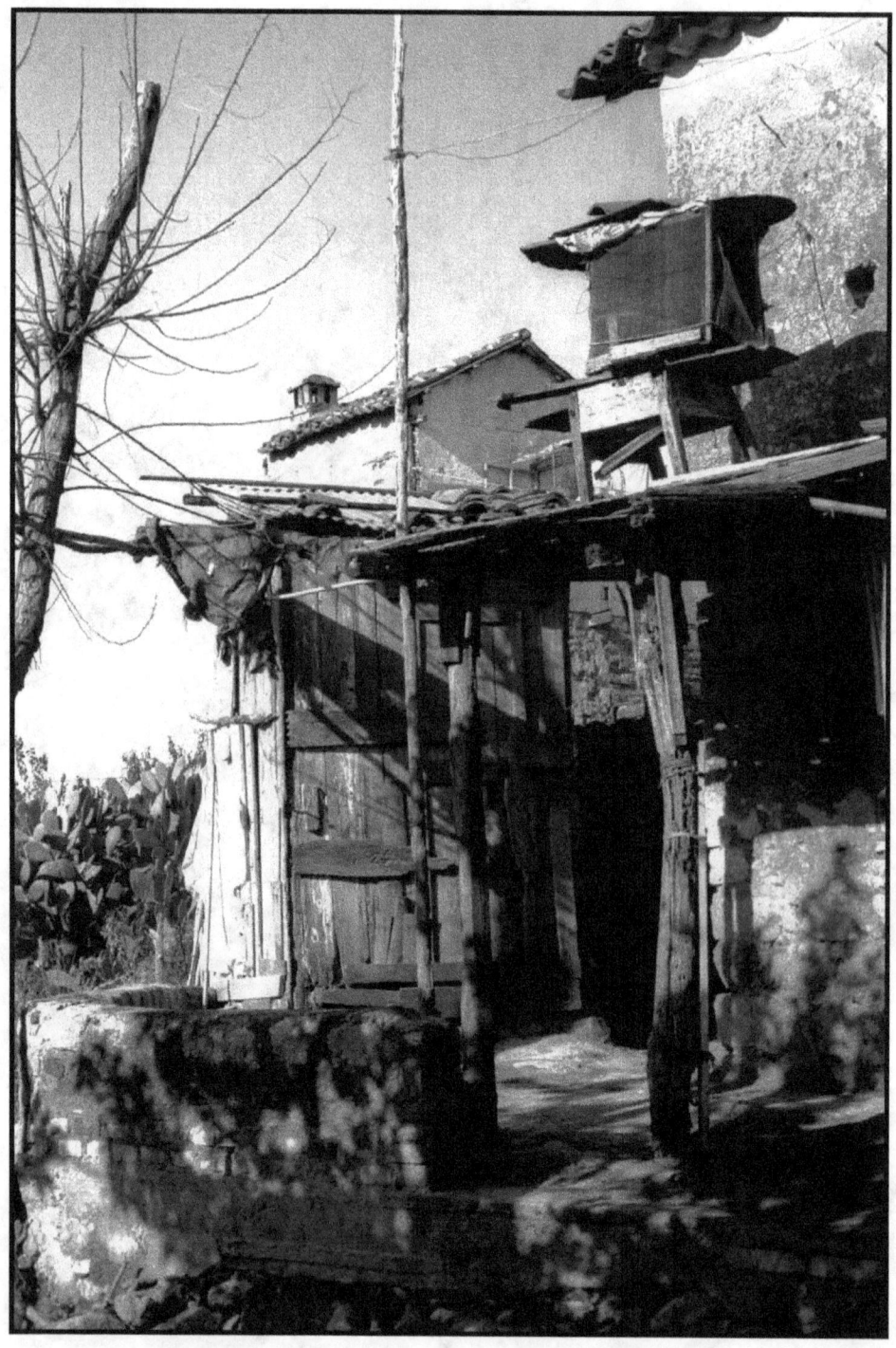

1972 – Limpidi (VV) – Abandoned houses – Olympus OM1 – Devel. Ilford FP4

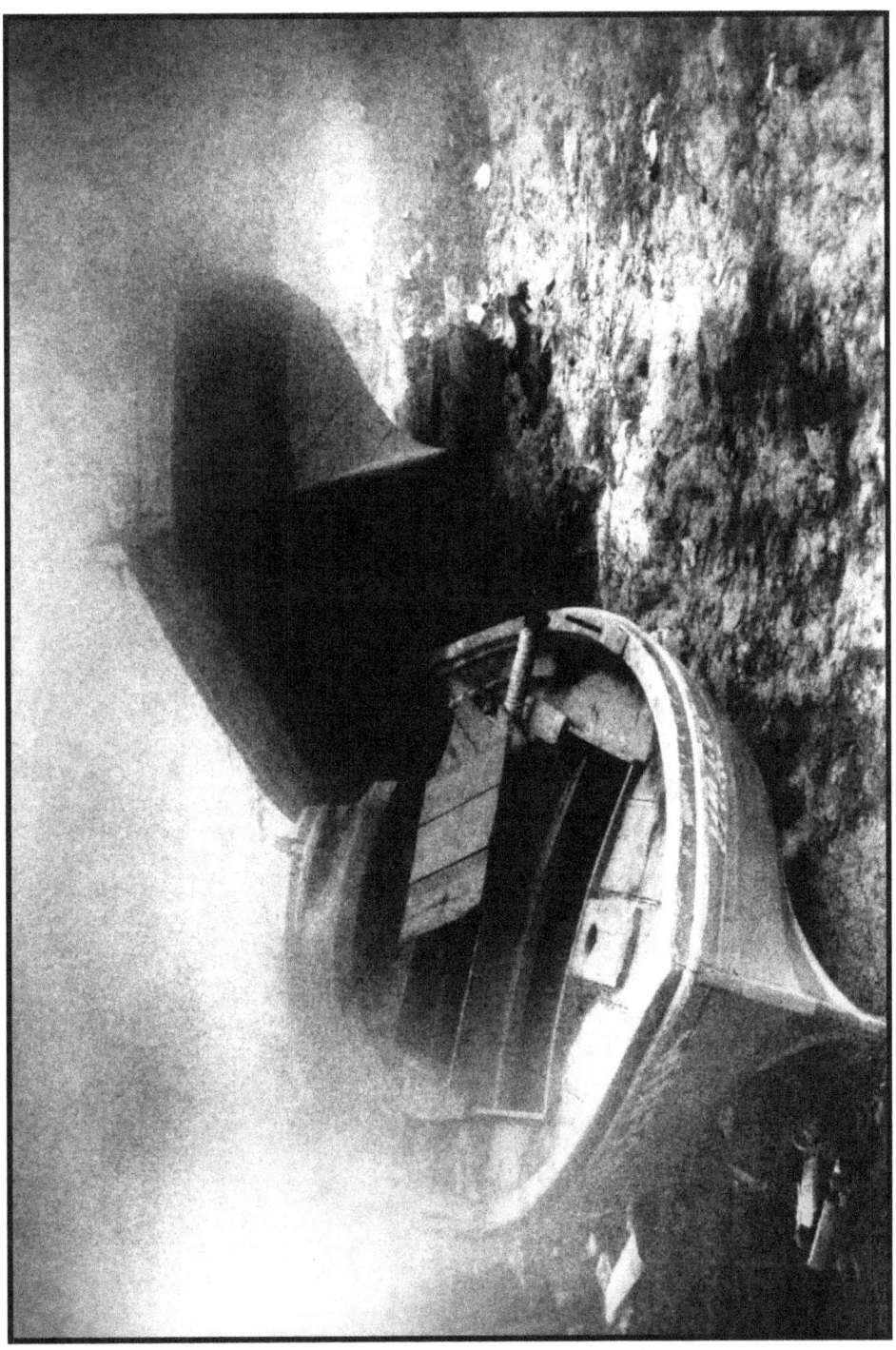

1971 – Briatico (VV) – Boats - Yashica FX3 - Ilford HP 400 - Devel. Rodinal

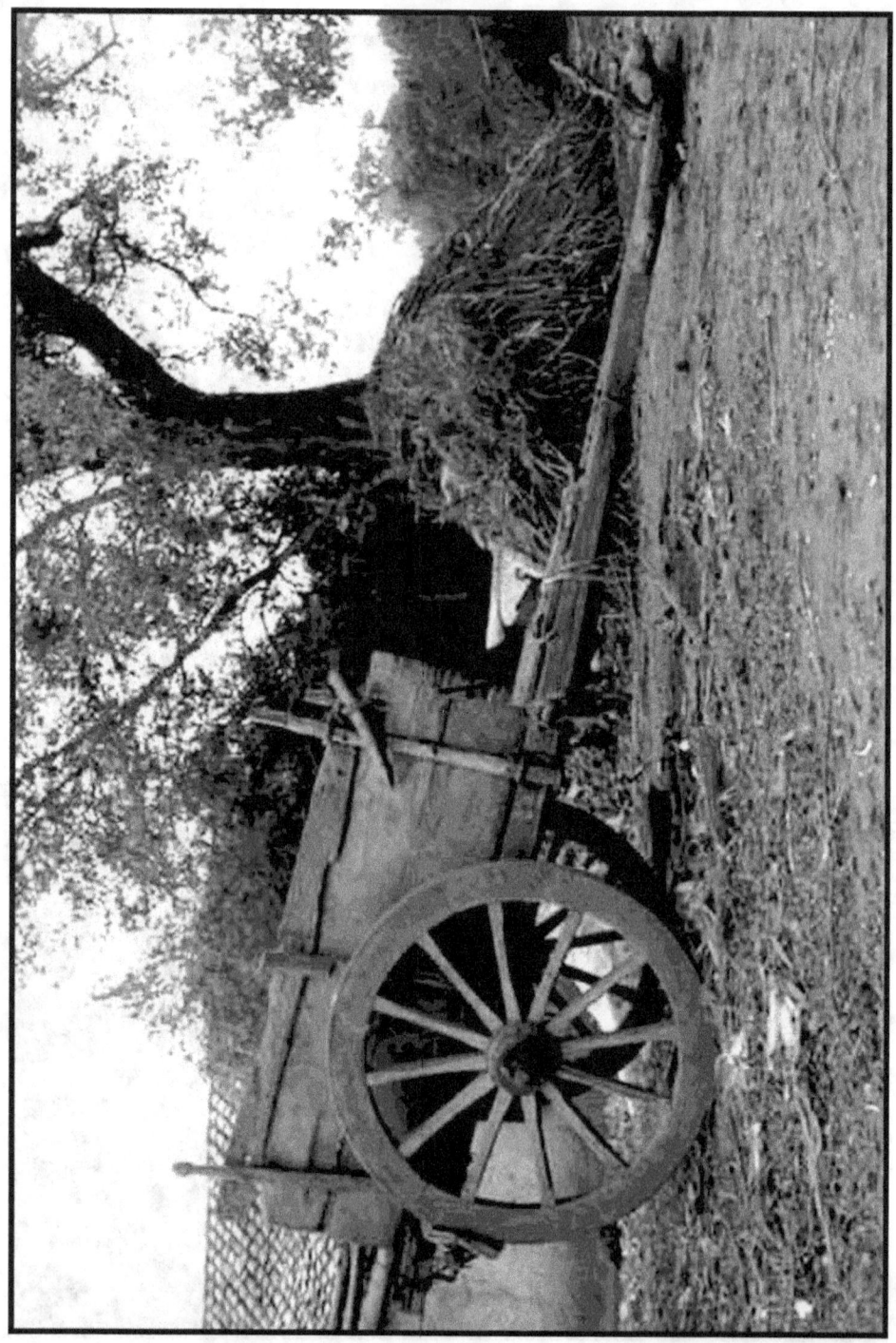

1971 – S.Onofrio (VV) - Barrow – Yashica FX3 - Ilford FP4 - Devel. Microphen

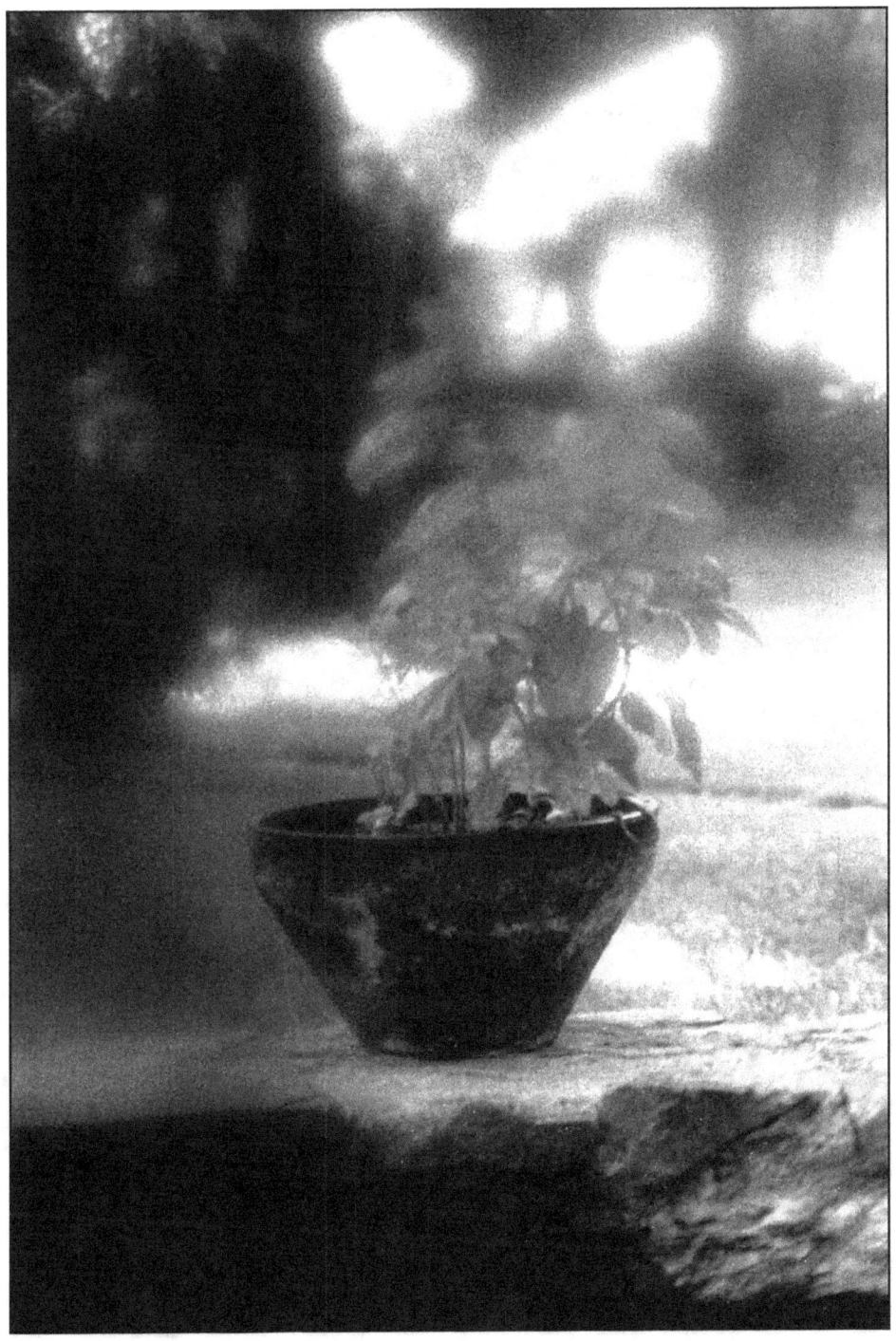

1985 – Plant - Olympus OM1 - Ilford FP4 - Devel. Microphen

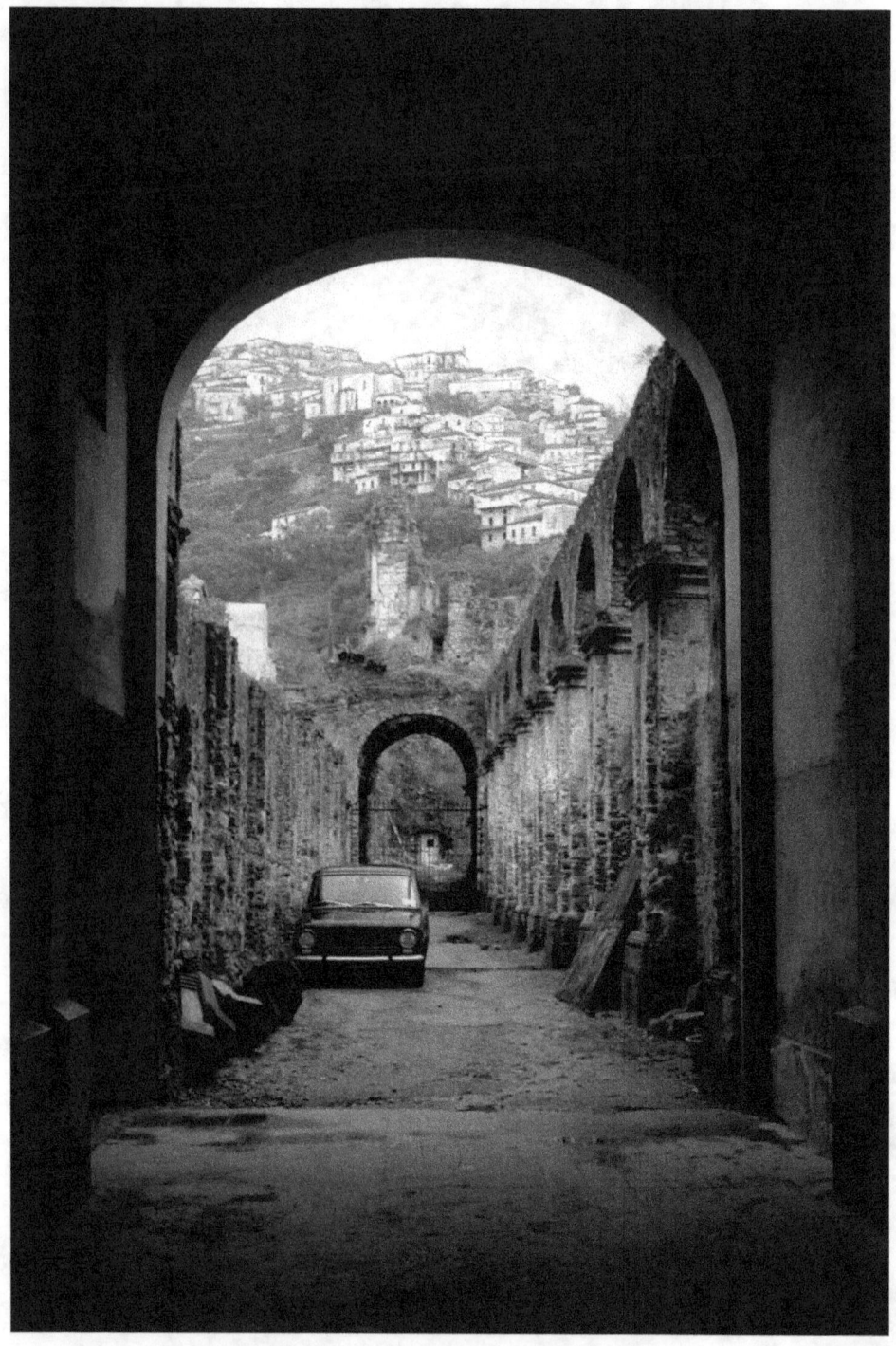

1971 – Soriano (VV) - Ancient convent – Yashica FX3 - Ilford FP4 - Devel. Microphen

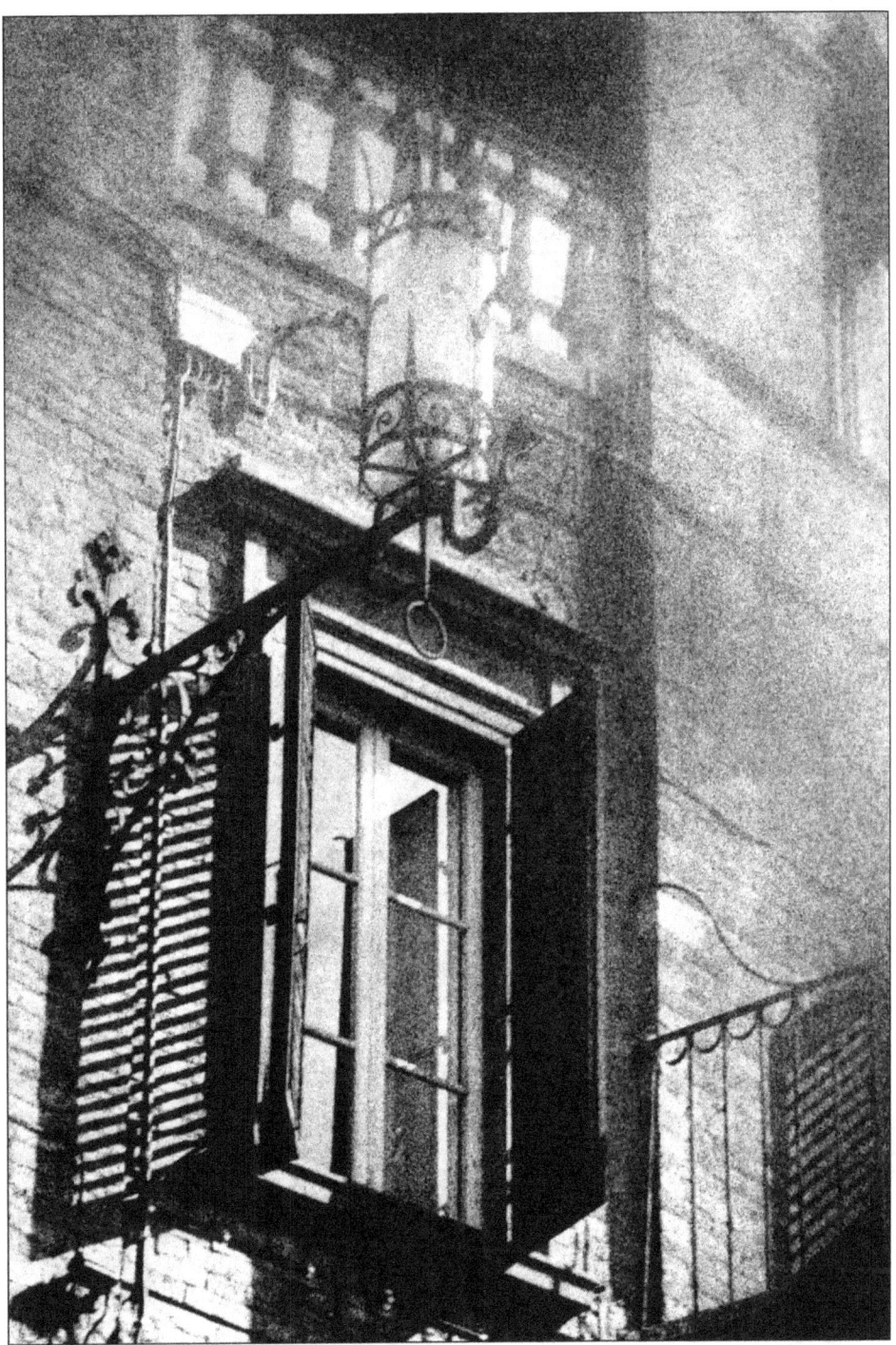

1973 – Siena - Piazza del Campo window – Minolta XD - FP4 - Devel. Rodinal

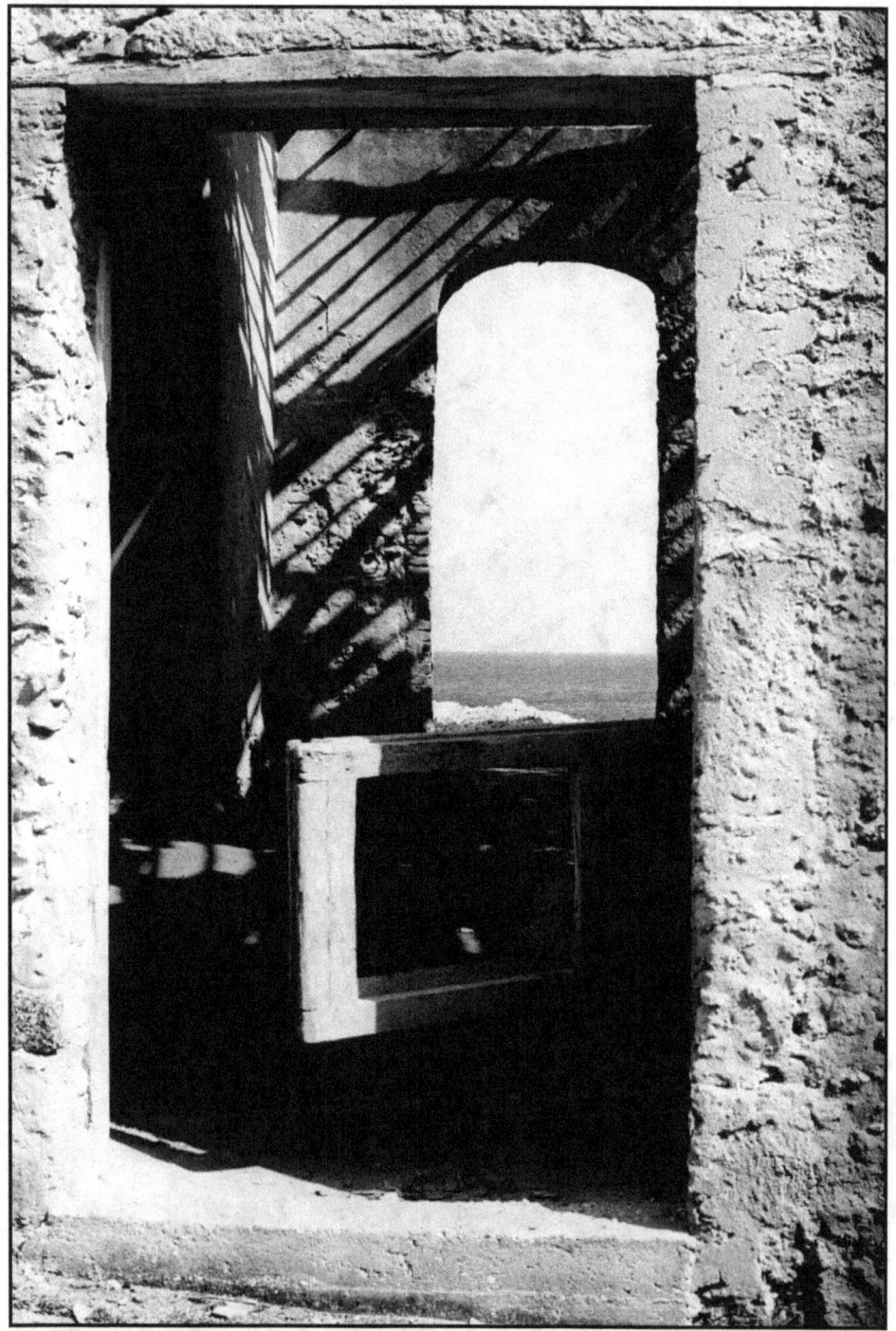
1985 – Abandoned house door - Olympus OM1 - Ilford FP4 – Devel. Microphen

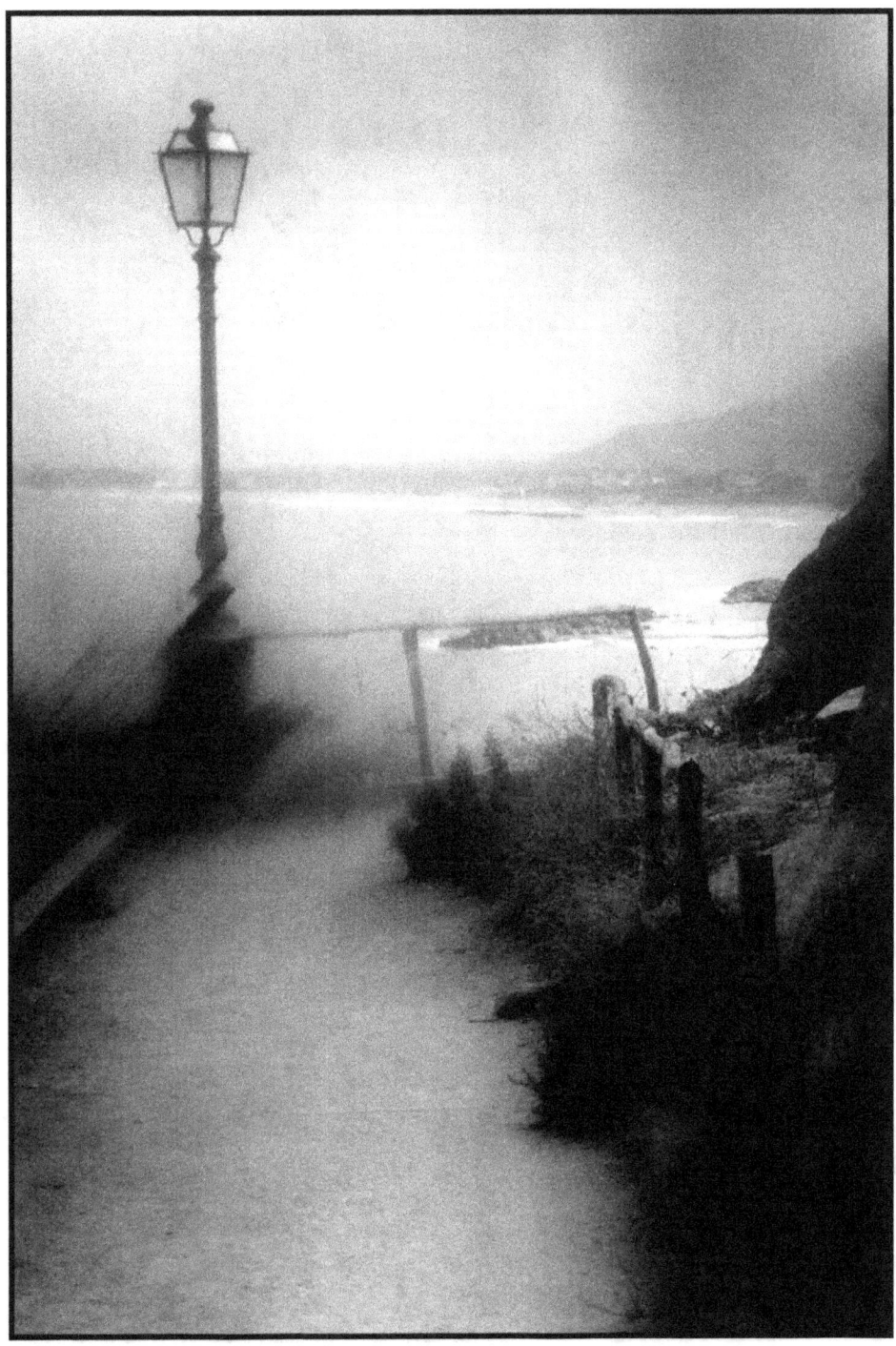

1980 - Sea view of Pizzo Calabro - **Olympus OM1** - **Ilford FP4** – Devel. Microphen

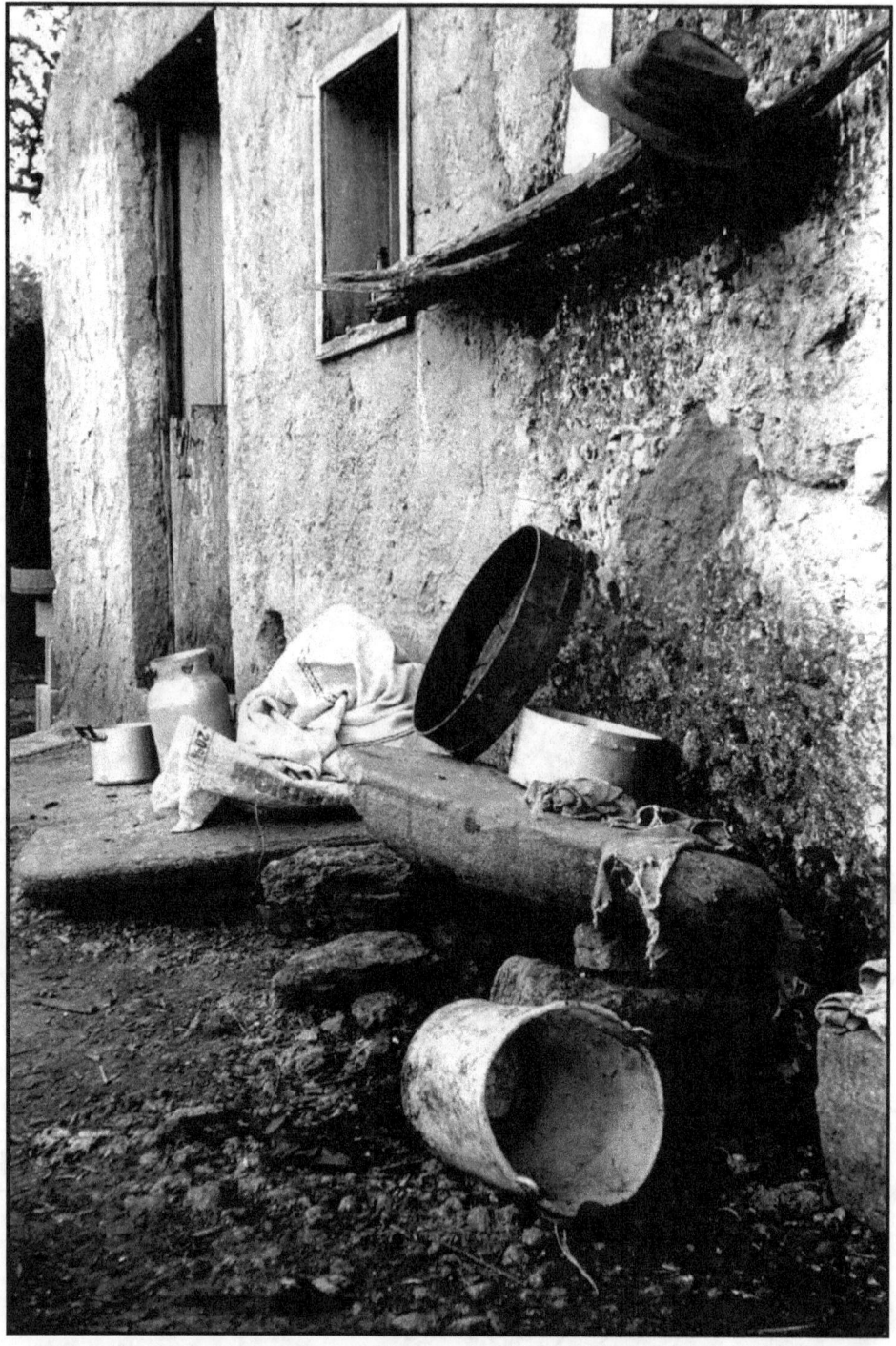

1985 – S. Onofrio (VV) - Peasant house – Olympus OM1 - Ilford FP4 – Devel. Microphen

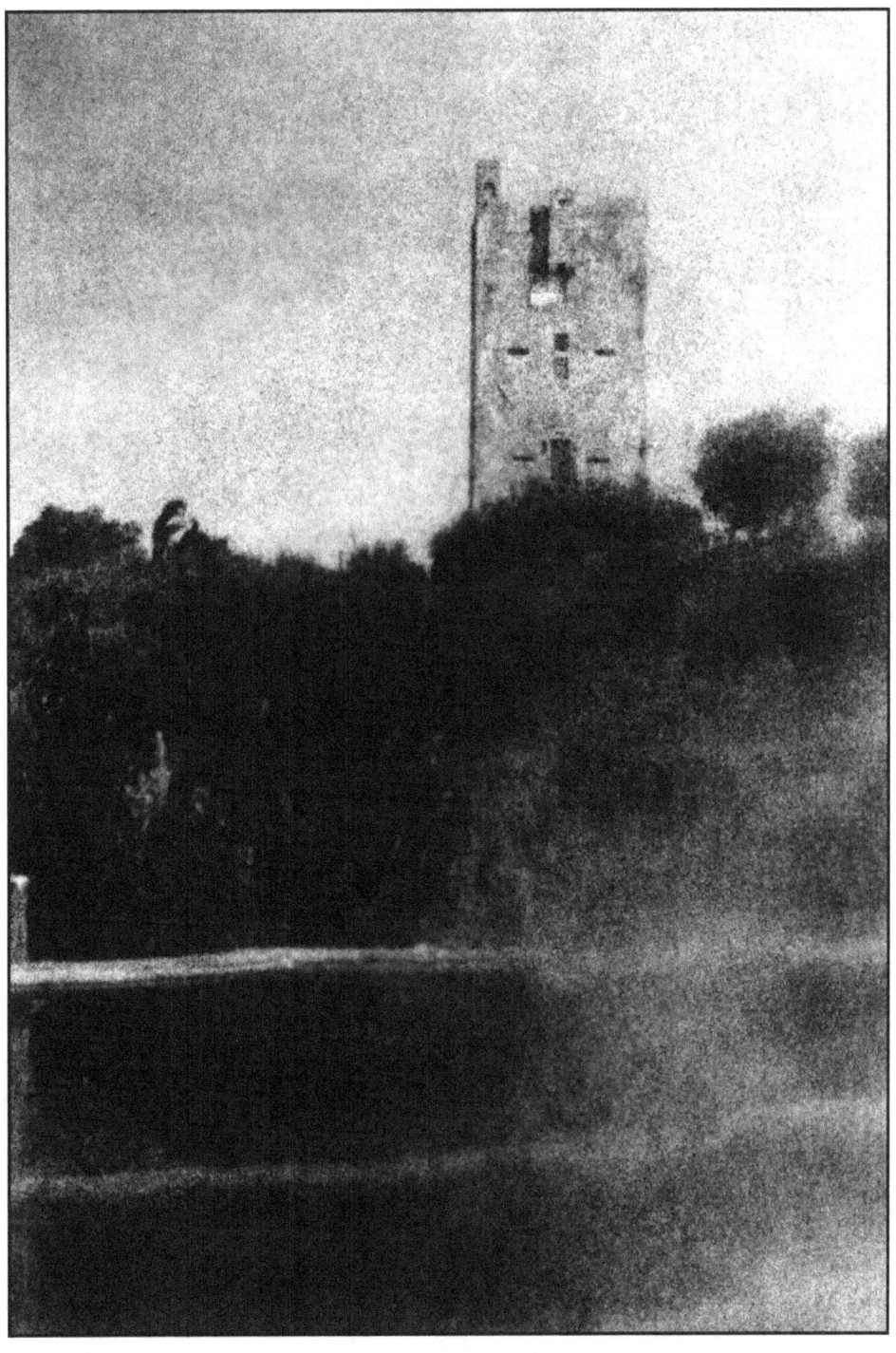

1973 – Punta Ala (Gr) – Idalgo Tower - Minolta XD - FP4 - Devel. Rodinal

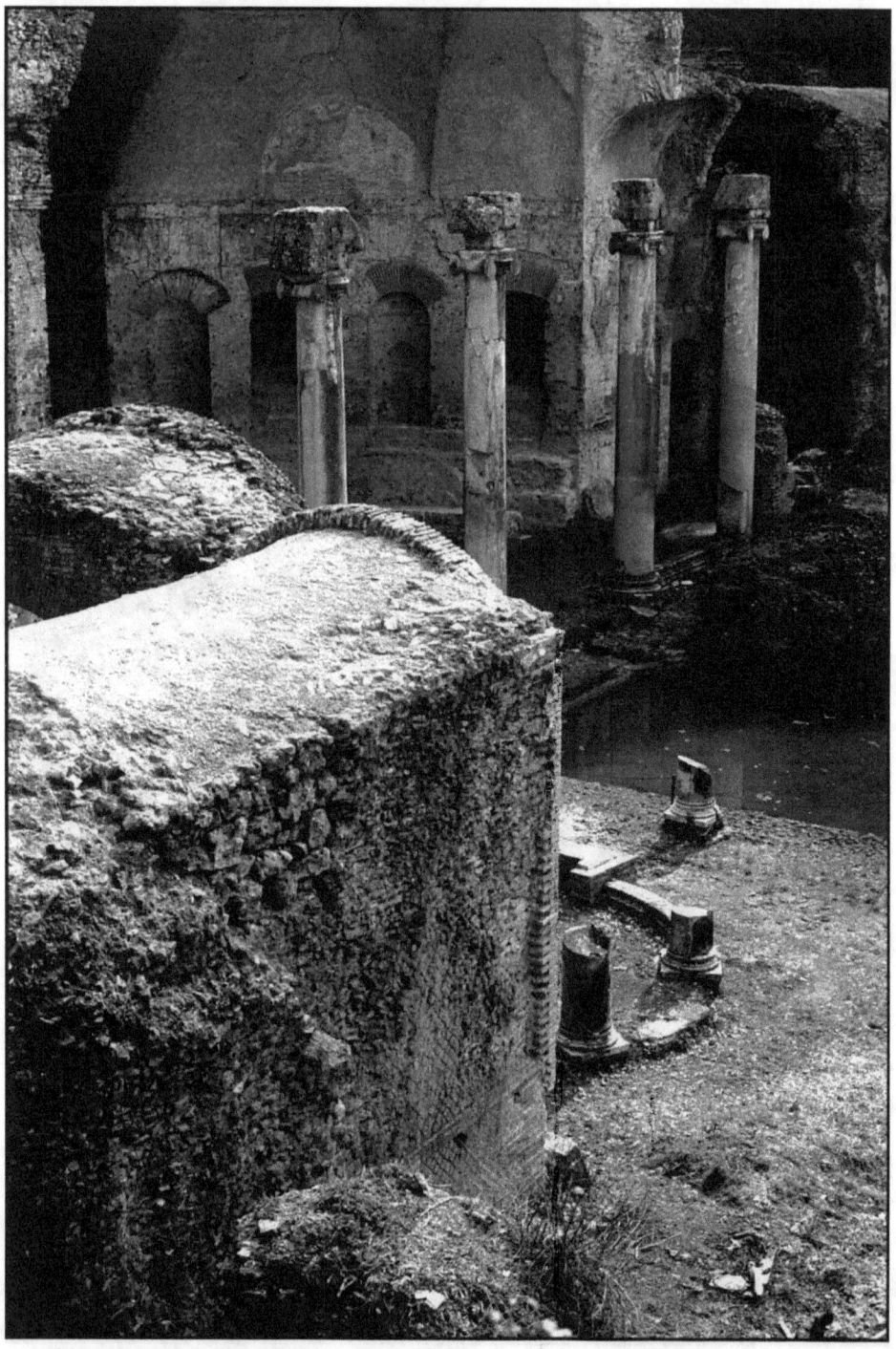

1985 – Tivoli - Villa Adriana - Olympus OM1 - Ilford FP4 – Devel. Microphen

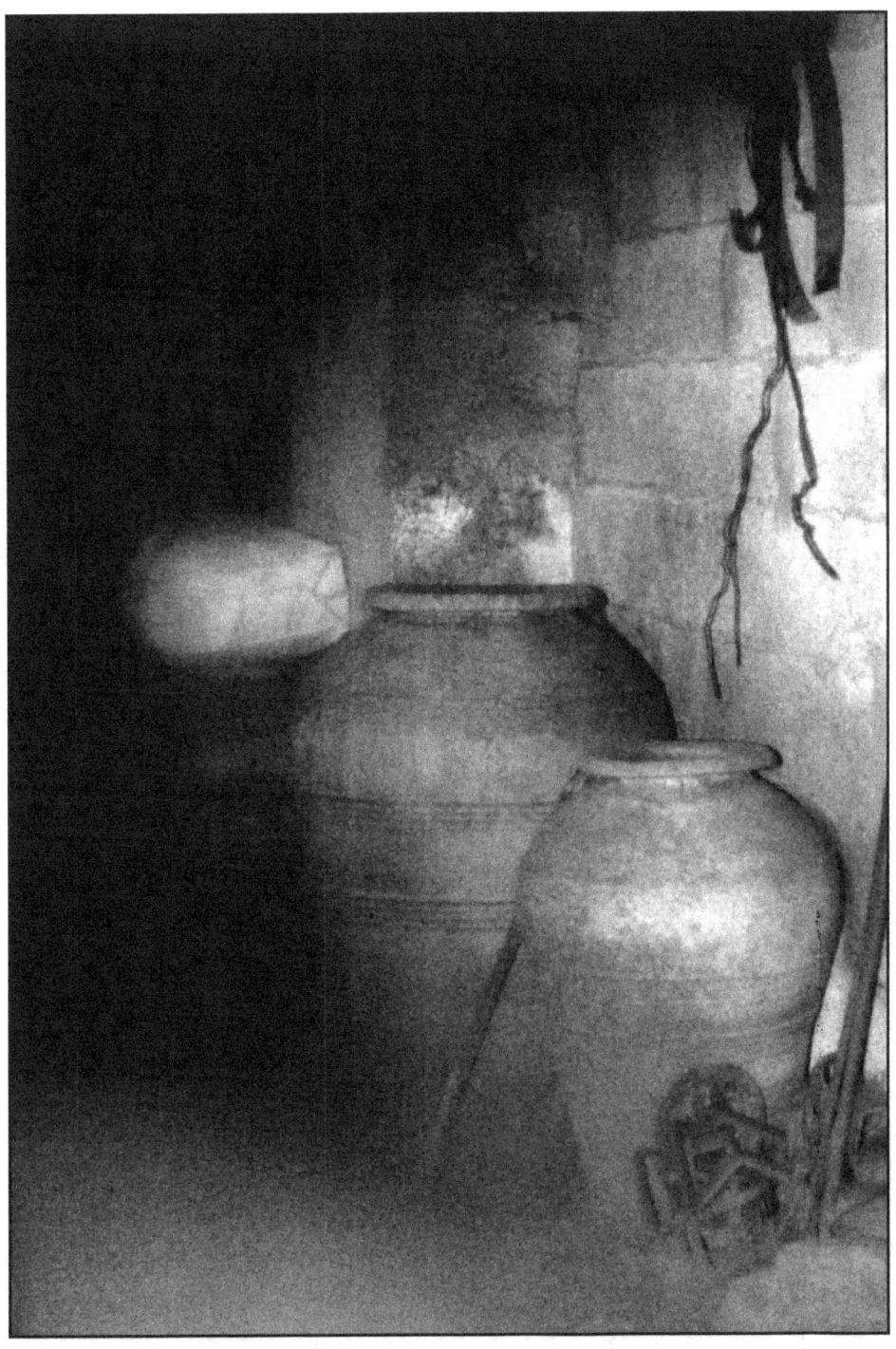

1973 – Jars - Minolta XD - FP4 - Devel. Rodinal

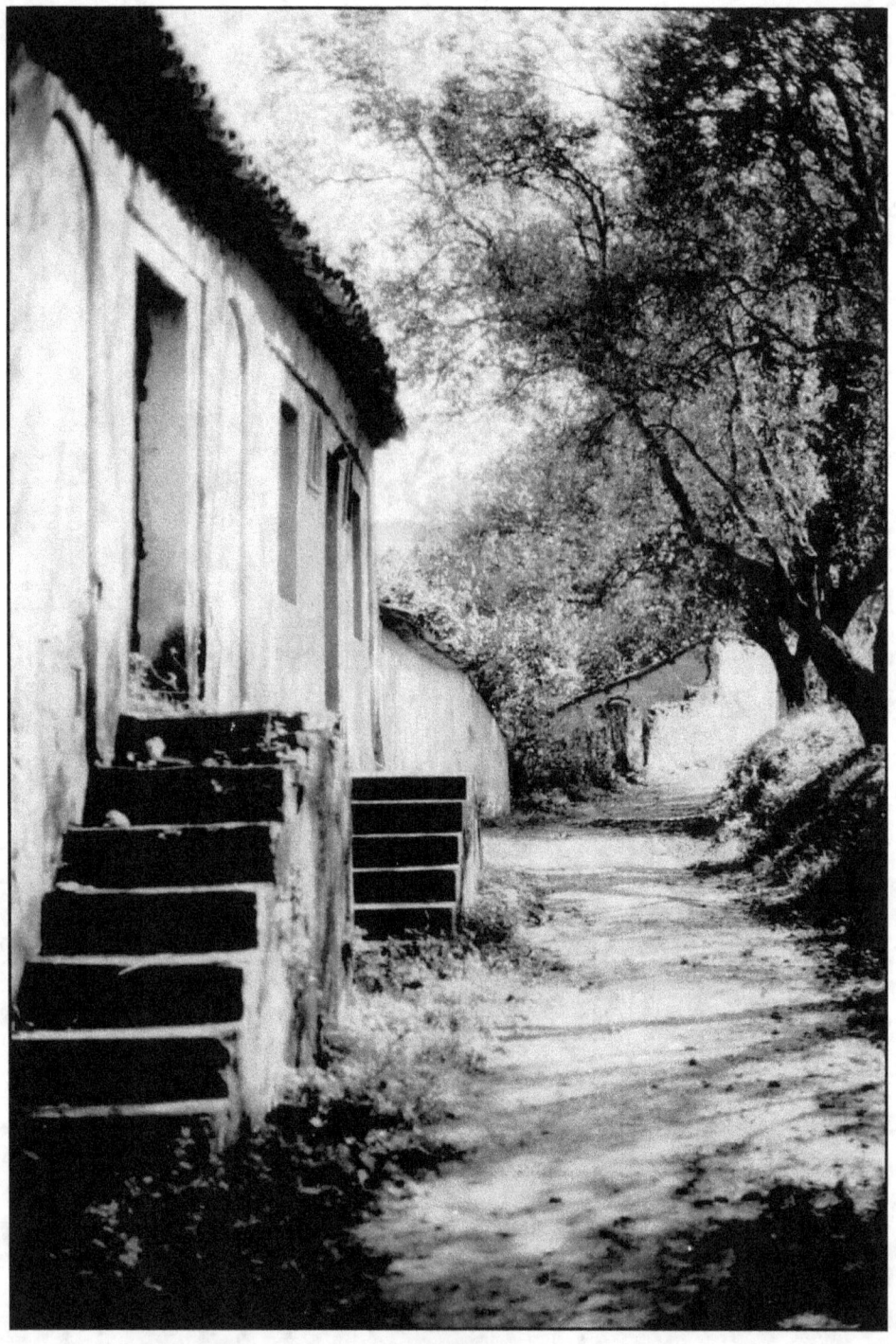

1973 – Abandoned houses - Minolta XD - FP4 – Development. Microphen

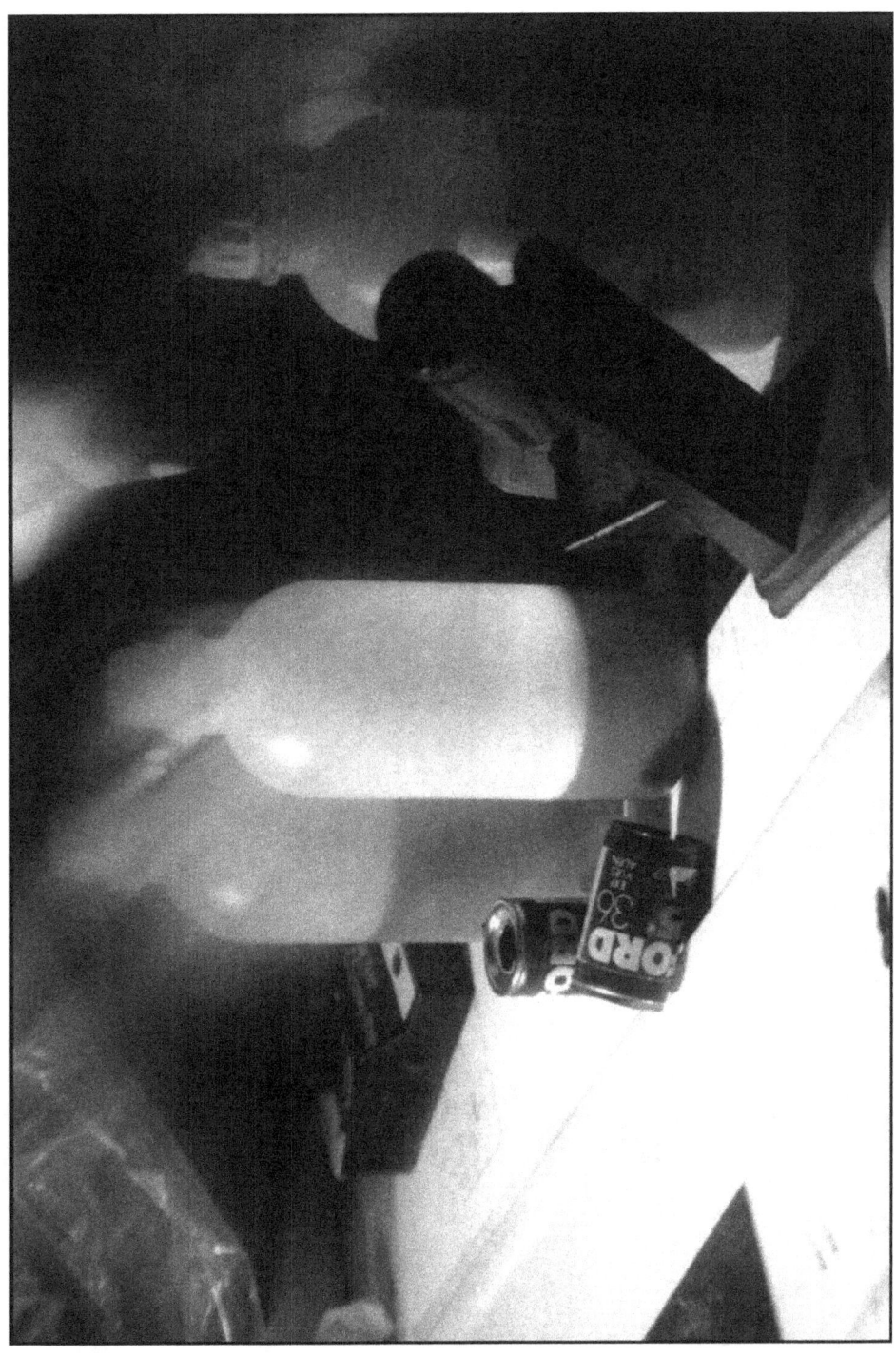

1971 – Darkroom objects - Yashica FX3 - Ilford FP4 – Devel. Microphen

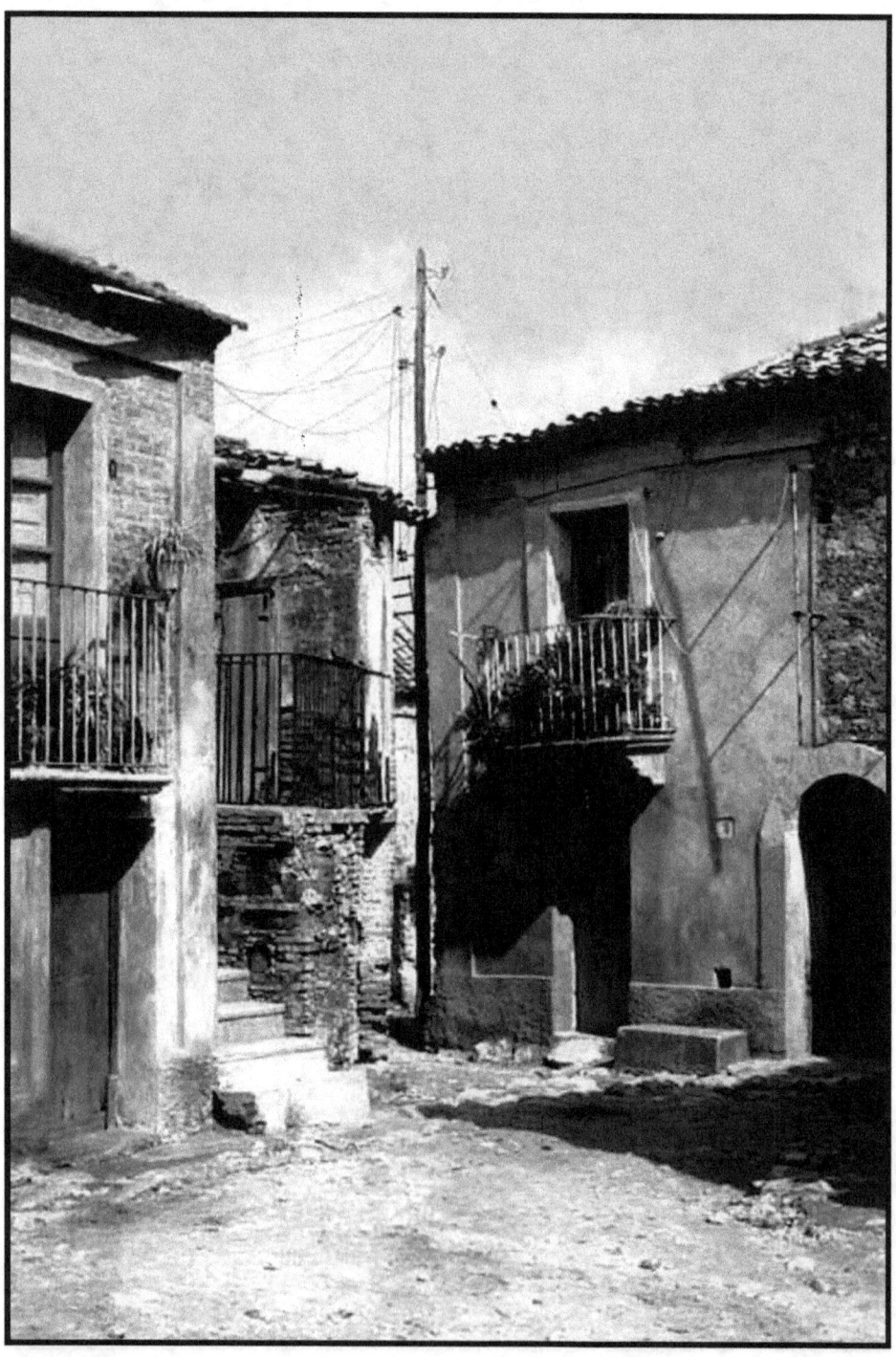
1972 – Papaglionti (VV) - Country houses - Yashica FX3 - Ilford FP4 – Devel. Microphen

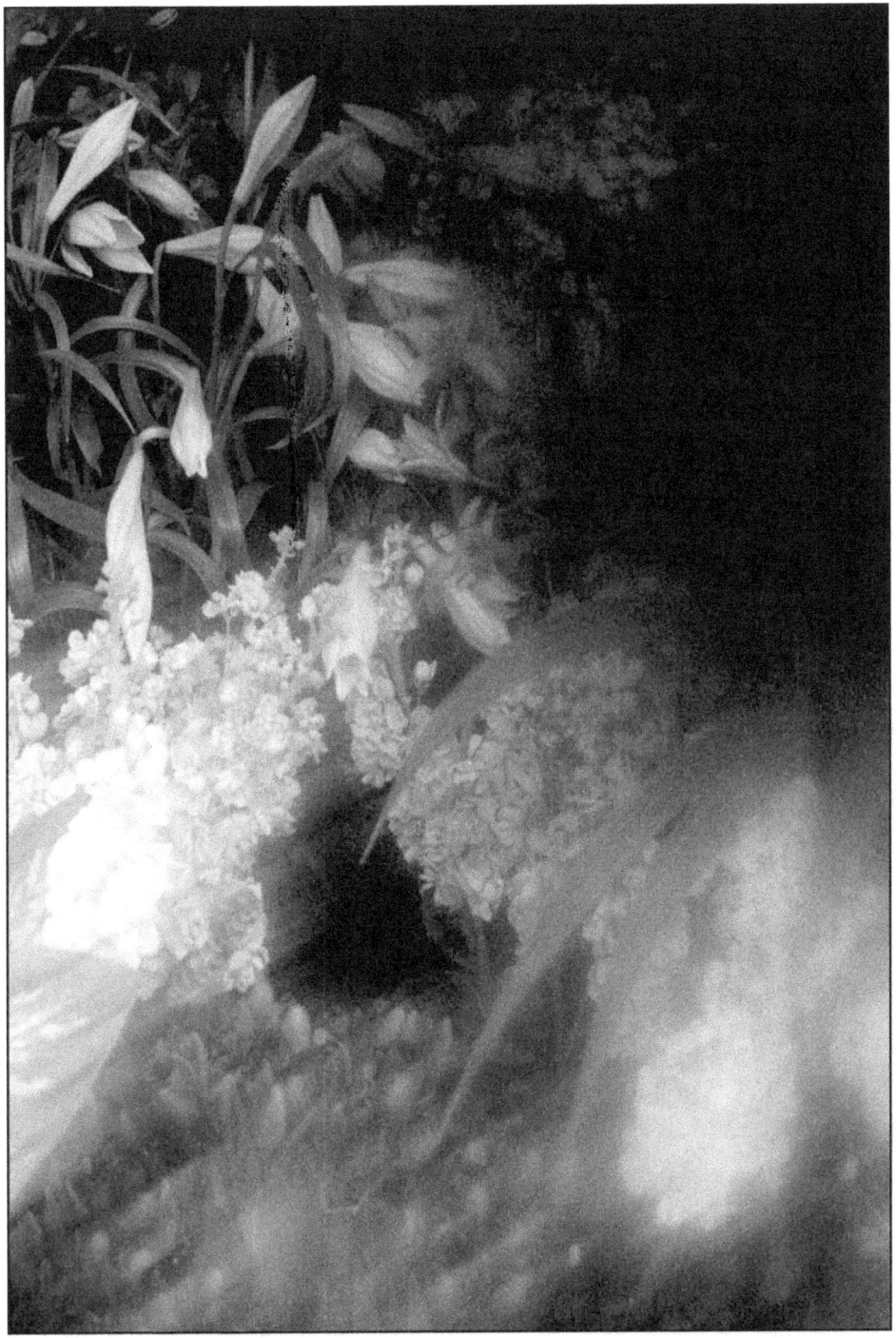

1982 - Flowers - Olympus OM2 - Ilford FP4 - Devel. D76

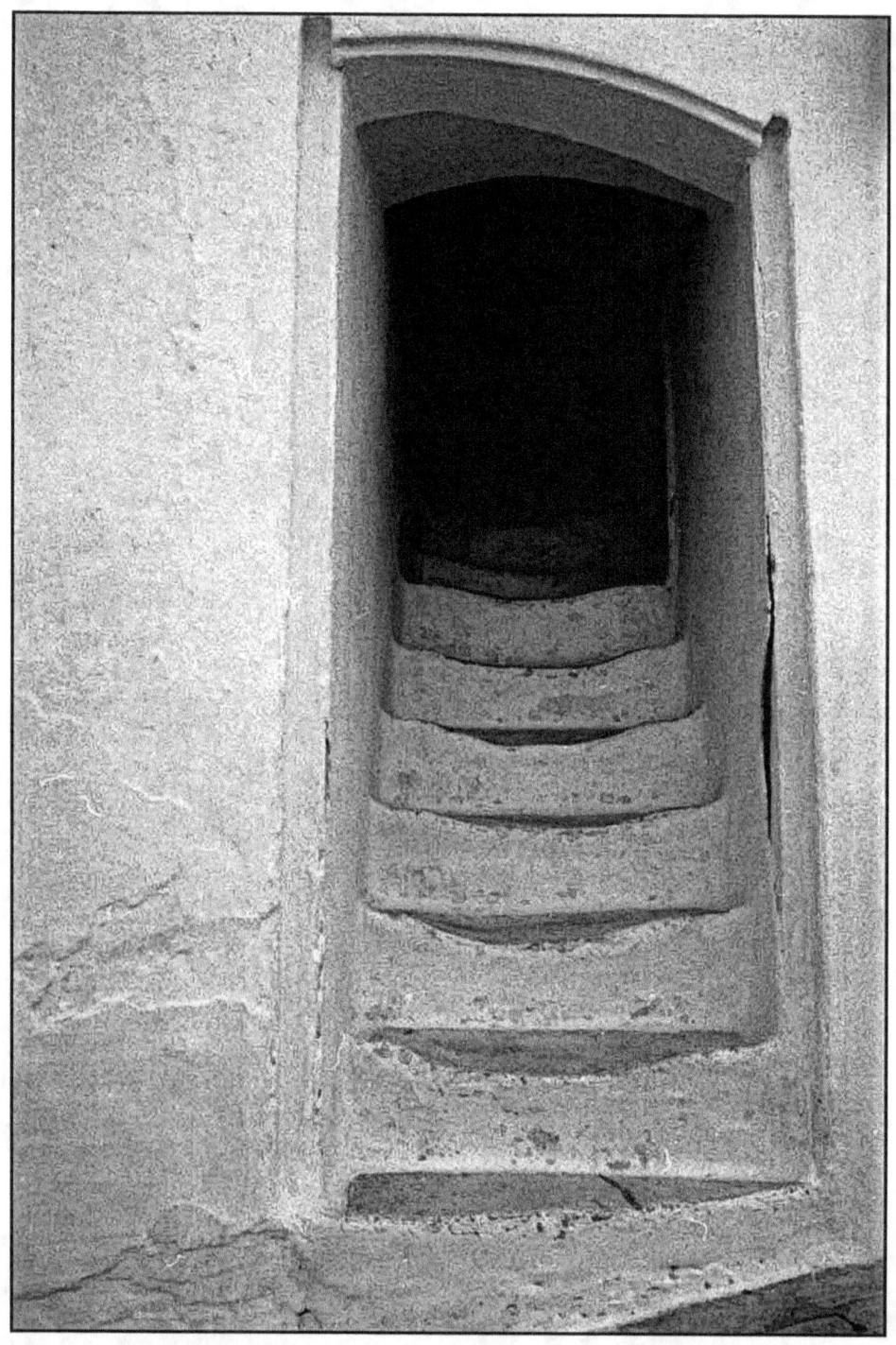

1977 - Aeolian Islands - Stairs - Minolta XD - FP4 - Devel. D76

FOTOART

*

6 VARIOUS PHOTOS

I have always sought to the beauty, the charm that inanimate things tacitly bring with them. Harmony always arose immediately after the moment of their presence was captured by the shot of my camera. Things and people have been an integral part of so many creative moments that the spirit first noticed stopping the time. Particular moment of unexpressed feeling, which carries within itself the silent harmony of the universe.

*

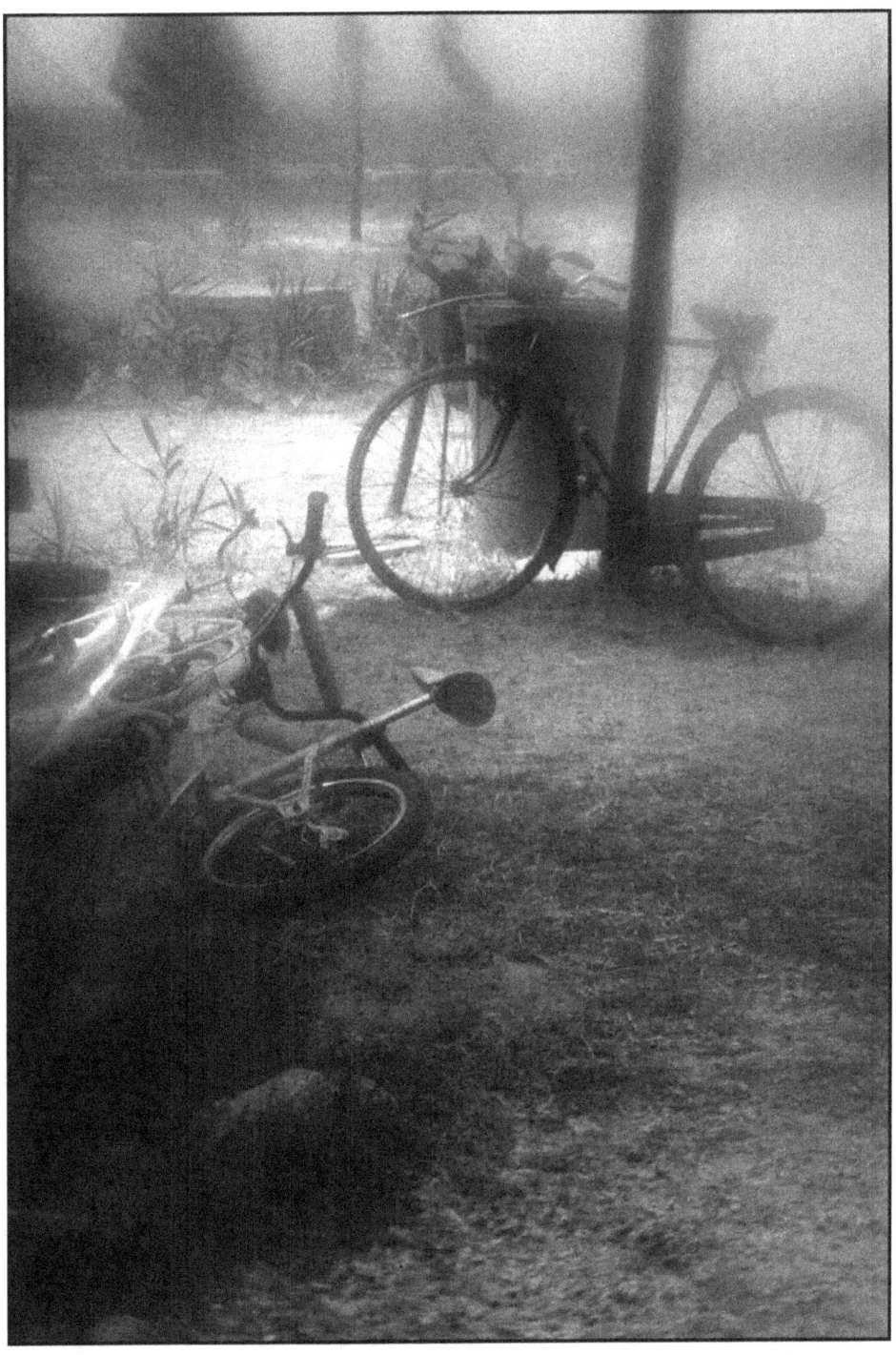

1971- Bicycles - Yashica FX3 - Ilford PAN F - Devel. Microphen

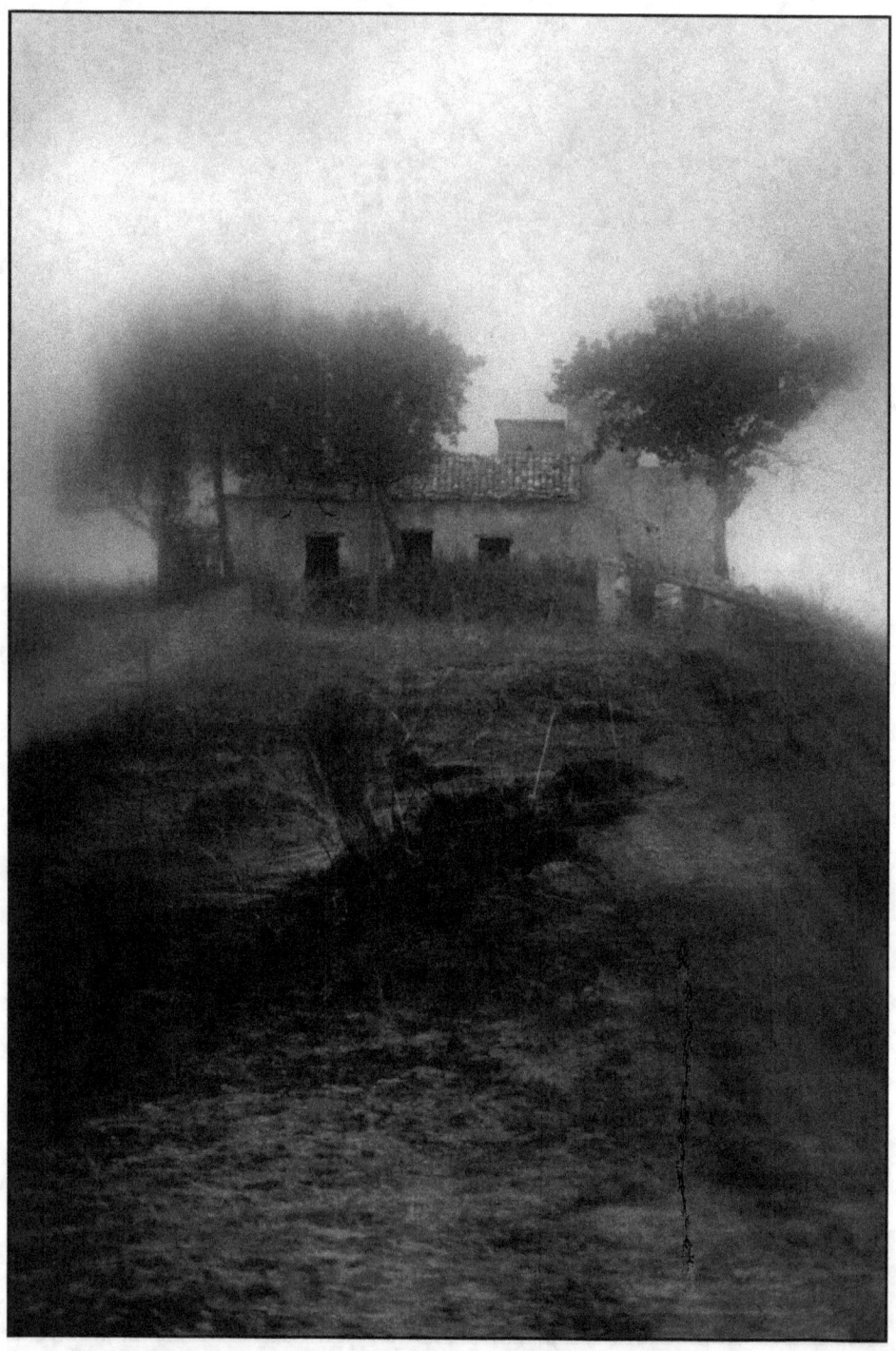

1980 - Country house - Minolta XD11 - Agfapan 100 - Devel. Microfen

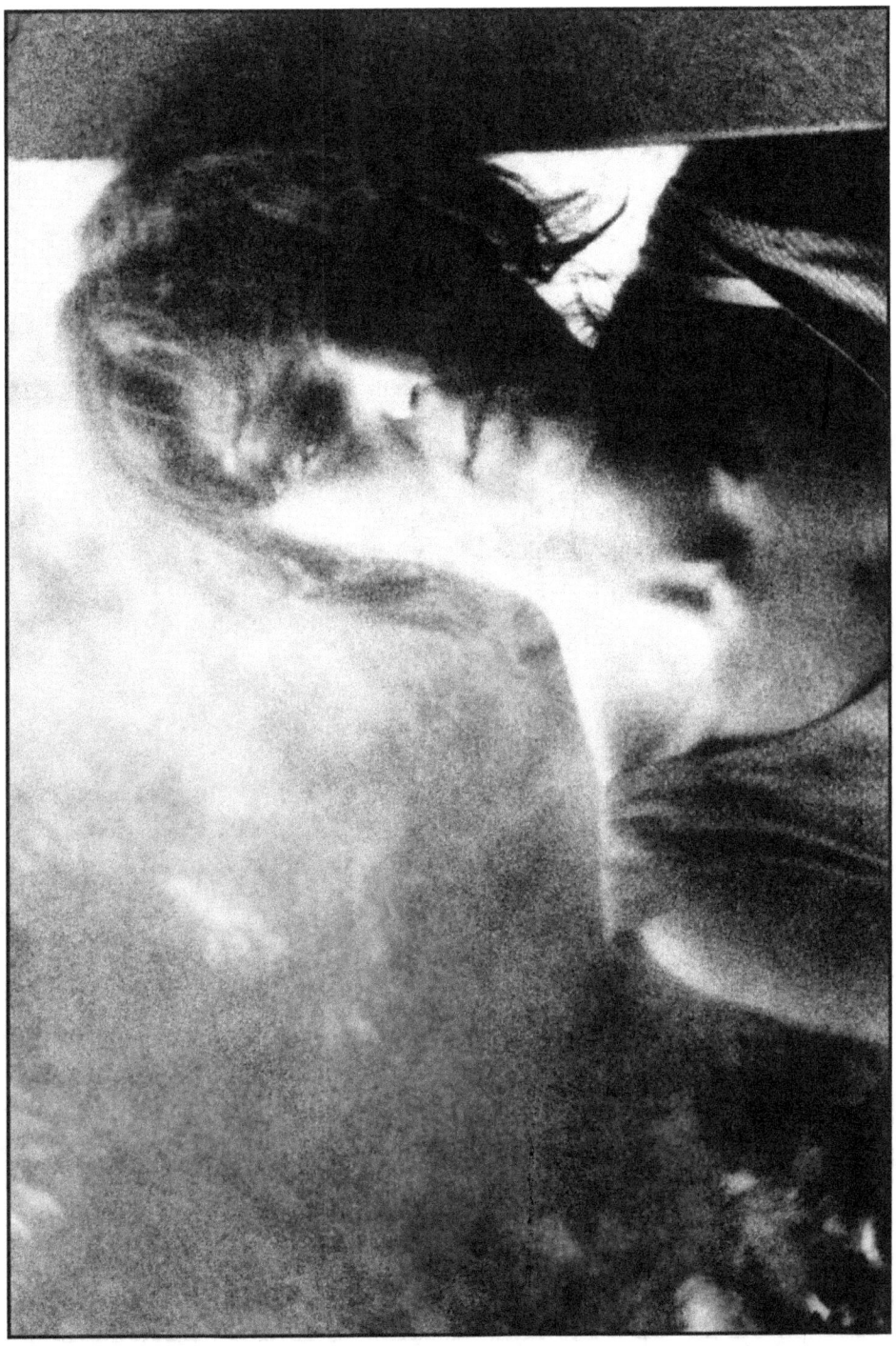

1980 - Portrait - Yashica FX3 - Agfapan 400 - Devel. Rodinal

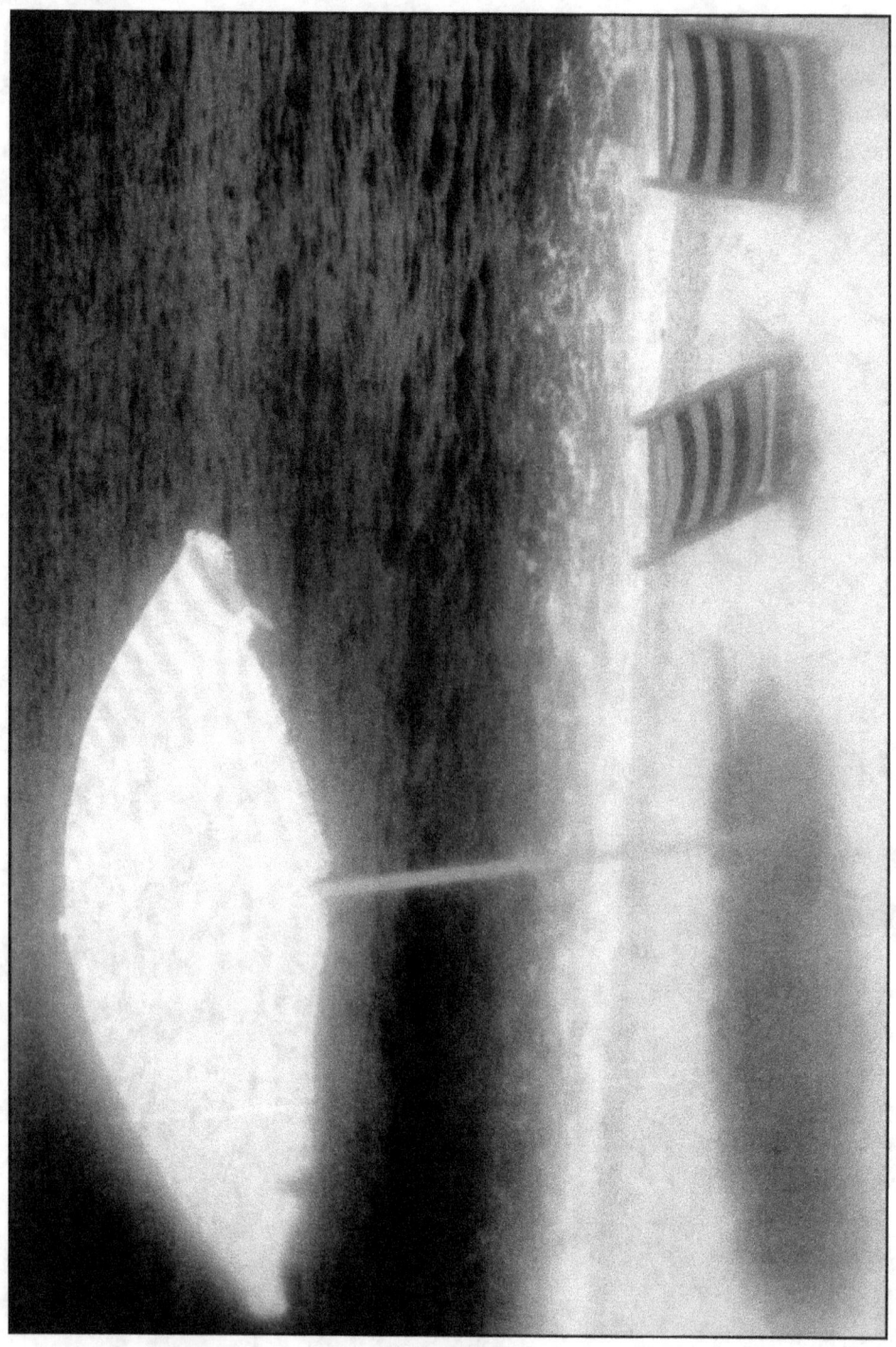

1984 - Beach umbrella - Yashica FX3 - PAN F - Devel. Microphen

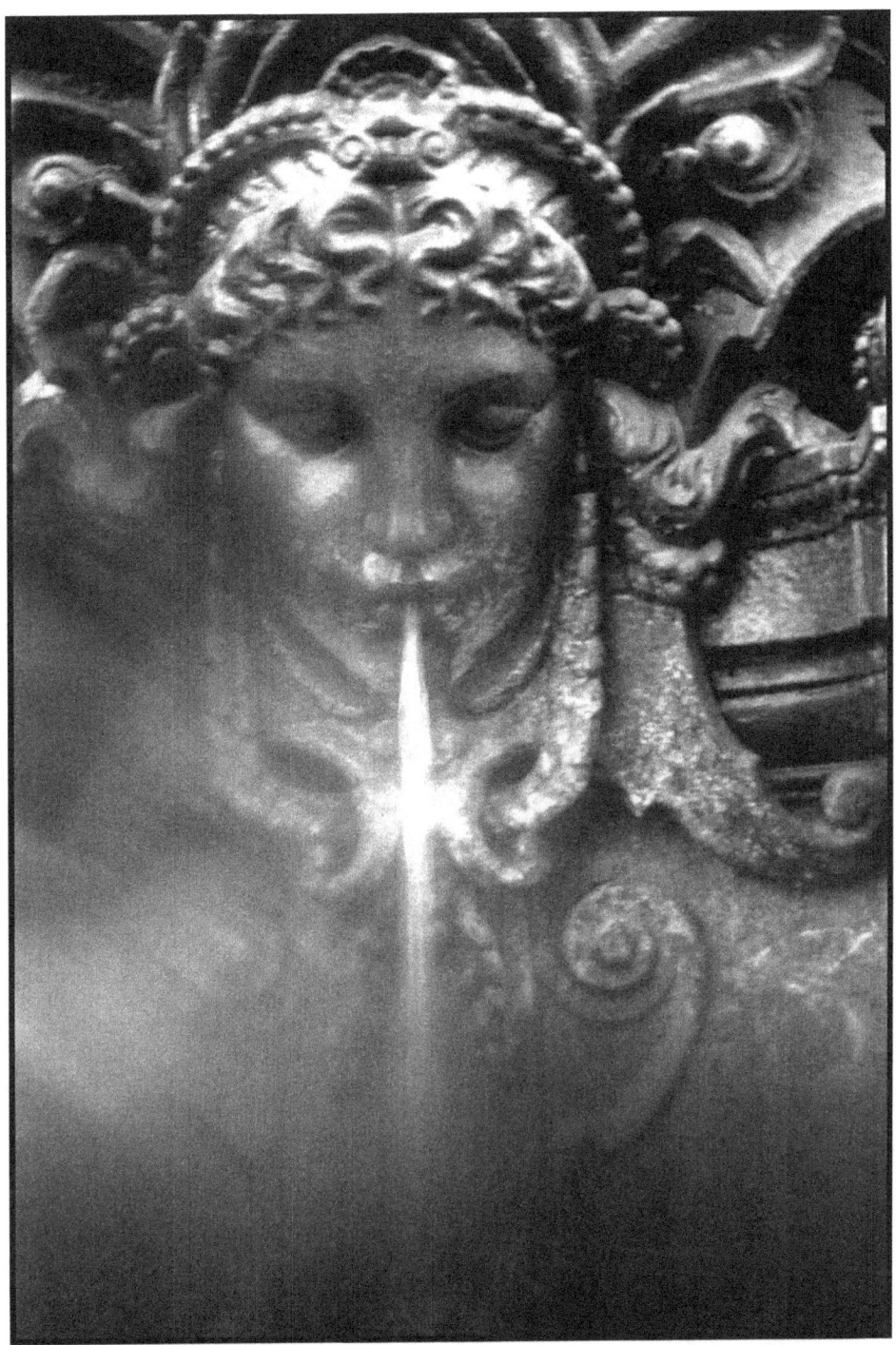

1984 – Paris - Fountain – Olympus OM1- Ilford FP4 - Devel. ID11

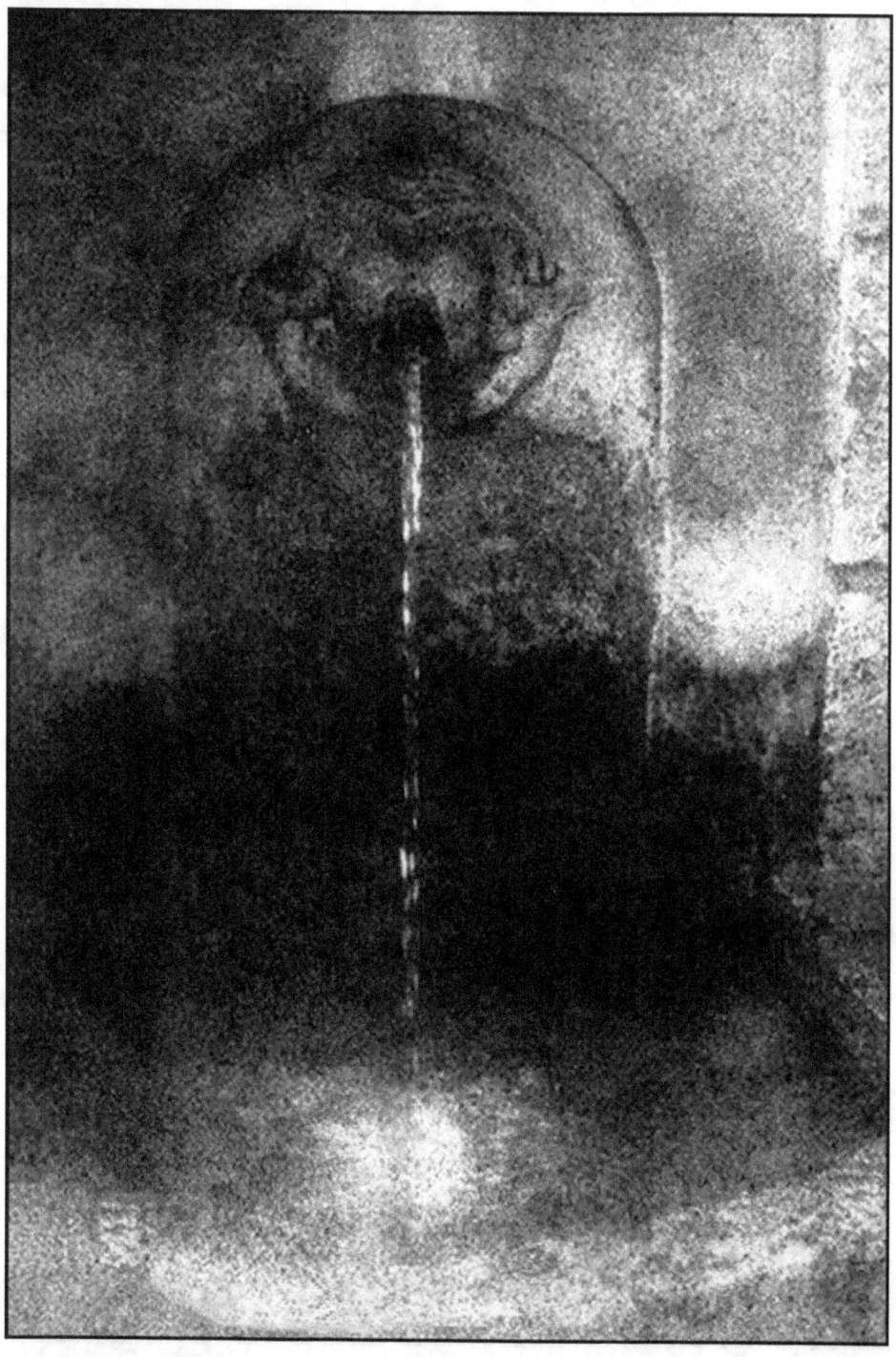

1978 - Fountain - Eura Ferrania - Ferrania P 3 - Devel done manually similar to Rodinal

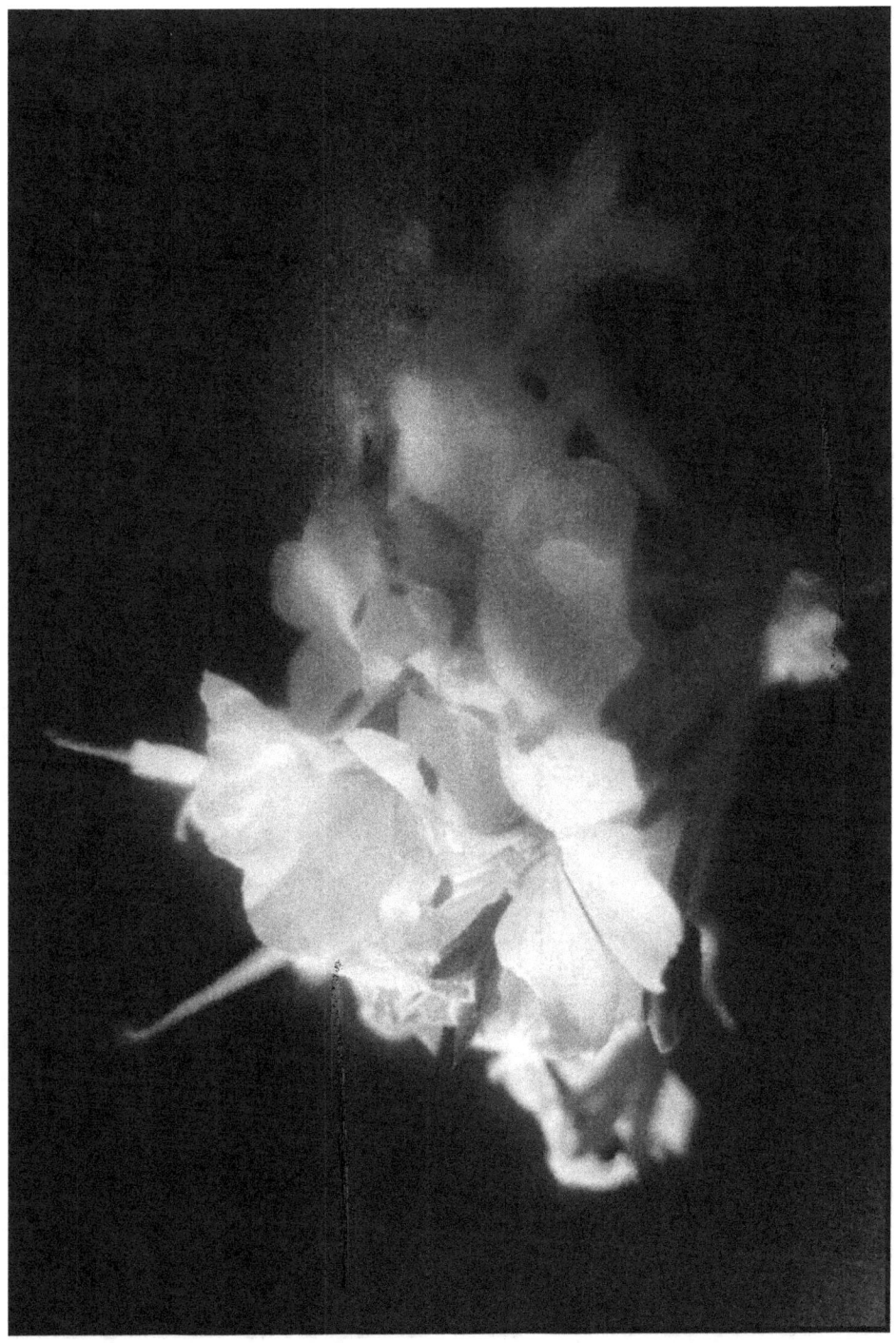

1980 - Geranium - Yashica FX3 - Ilford HP5 - Devel. Microphen

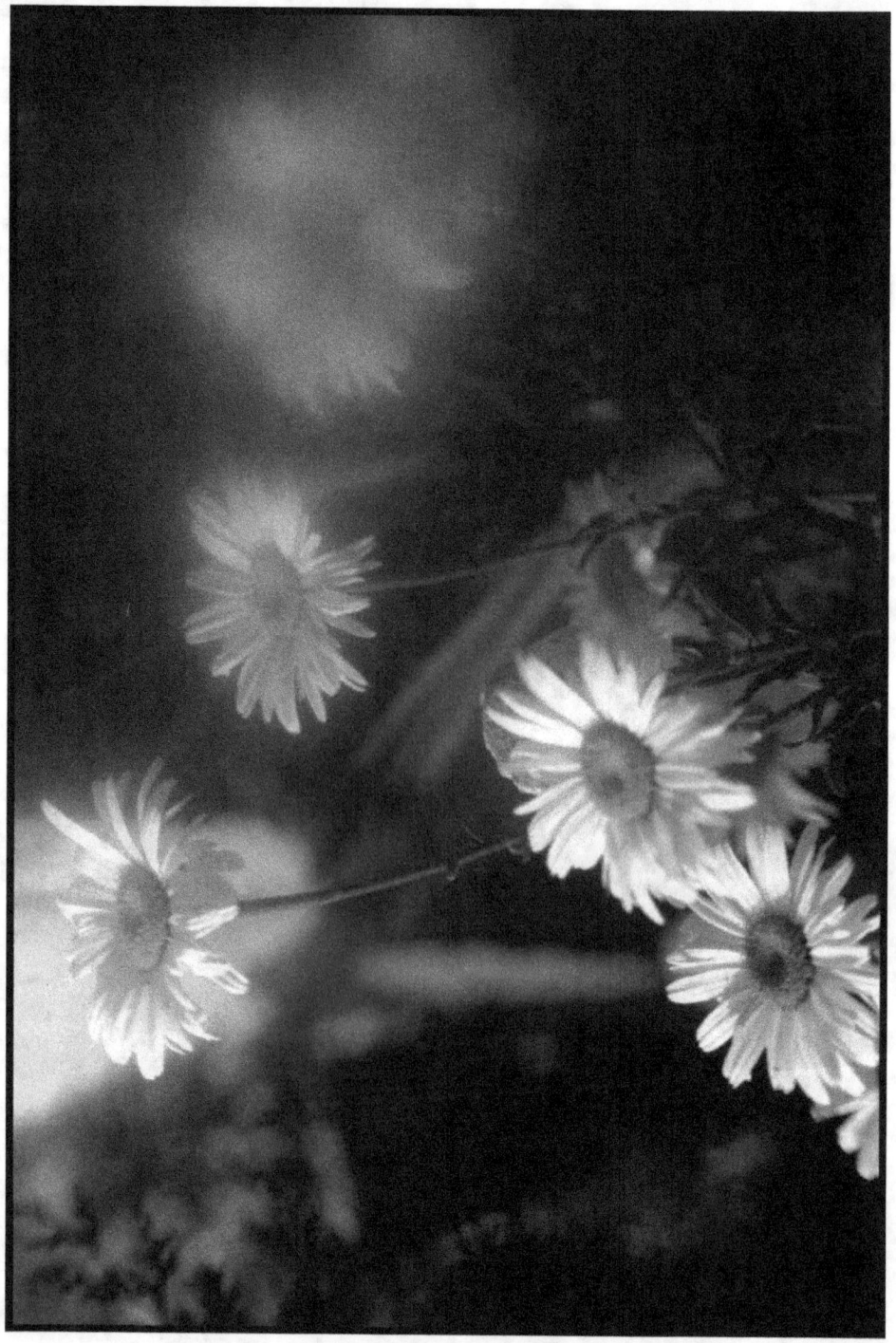

1980 - Daisies - Yashika FX3 - Ilford Pan F - Devel. Microphen

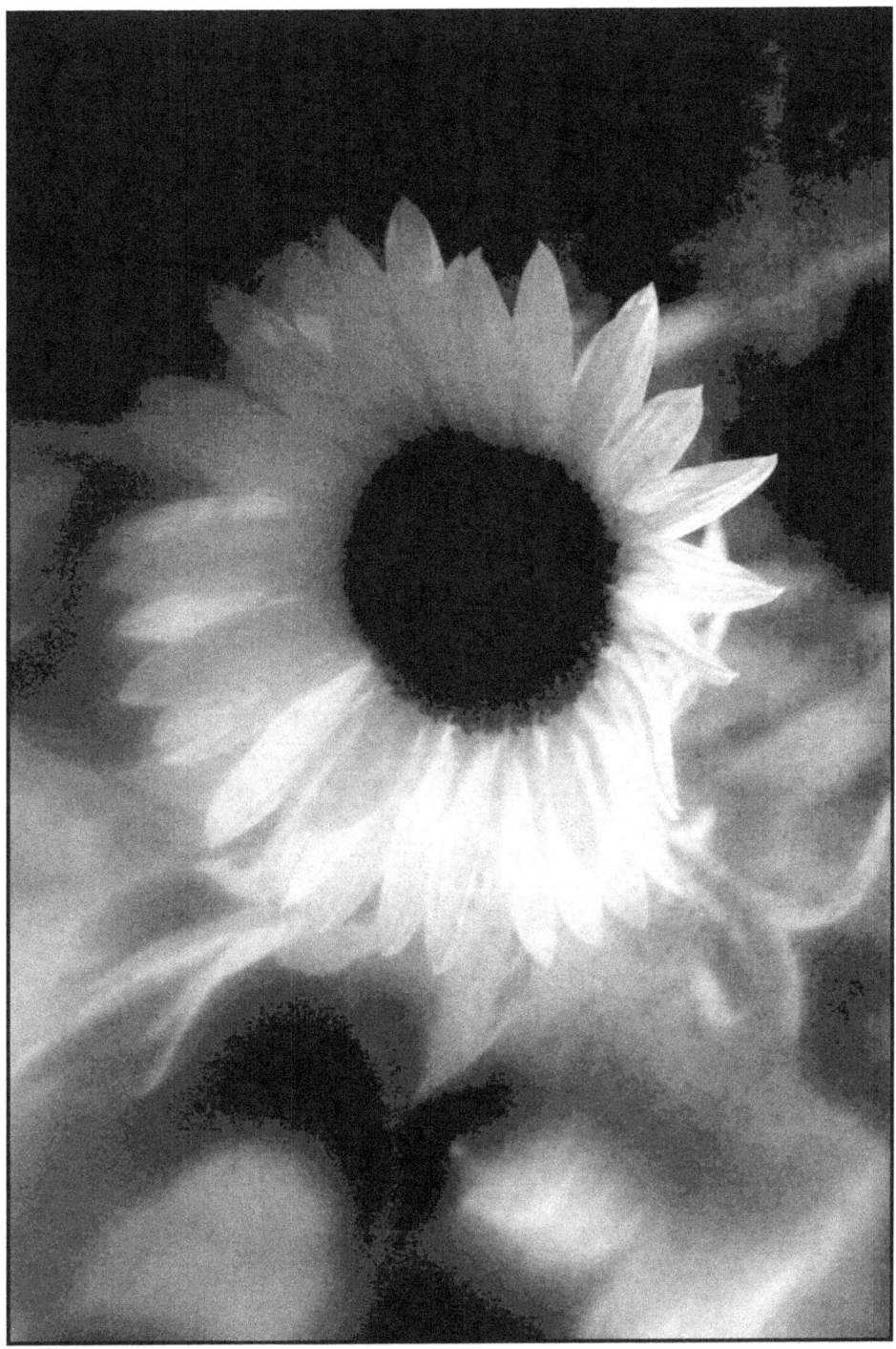

1980 - Daisy - Yashika FX3 - Ilford Pan F - Devel. Microphen

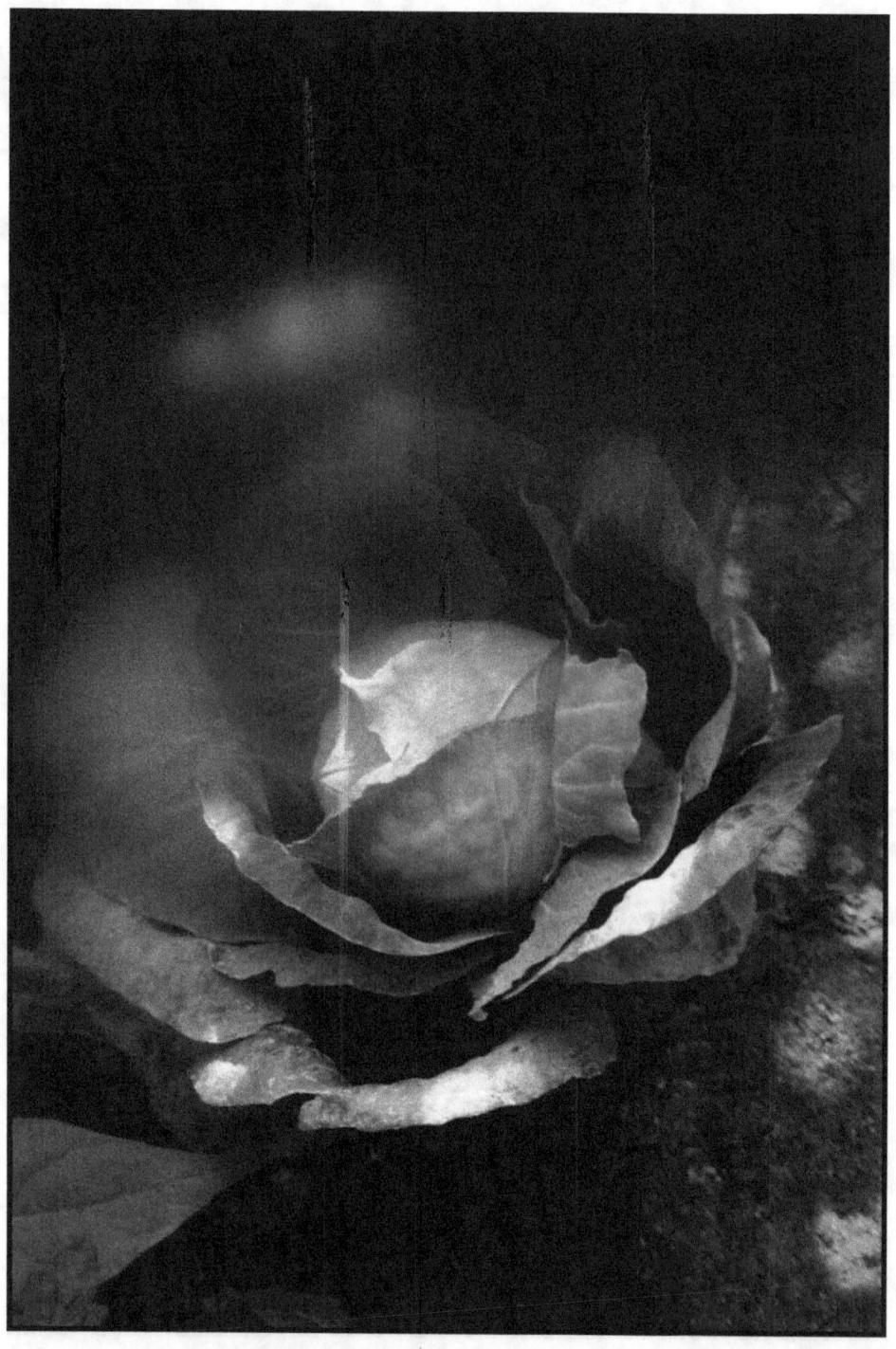

1980 - Cabbage - Yashica FX3 - Ilford PAN F - Devel. Microphen

FOTOART

FOTOART

*

7 AUTHOR INFORMATION

DOMENICO MURATORE

Born in Limpidi di Acquaro (VV.) on the 30th May 1948.
He attended the Vibo Valentia Classic High School and accomplished his high school diploma in 1967.
He graduated in Foreign Languages and Literature at the University of Messina.
He taught French Language and Literature at the Vibo Valentia Scientific High School and then, after moving to Milan, at the Commercial Technical Institute, until retirement.
His passions: research, photography and painting.
Today, he resides in Vibo Valentia.
Website: www.esoradionet.com
Published:
"Grammaire active de la langue Française" - Basic grammar of the French language for the two years of upper secondary school.
"Cahier d'exercices - Exercices par ordinateur" - Interactive French exercise book with software.
The wise:
"The myth of science in Sully Prudhomme"
"The path of science"
"What is Freemasonry"
"Modern practical magic"
Little stories:
"Tales from the fireplace"

www.ingramcontent.com/pod-product-compliance
Lightning Source LLC
Chambersburg PA
CBHW080502220526
45465CB00006B/2348